The Boxer Rebellion

CHINA, 1900

THE ARTISTS' PERSPECTIVE

Frederic A. Sharf
and
Peter Harrington

Greenhill Books, London

Stackpole Books, Pennsylvania

Greenhill Books

The Boxer Rebellion
CHINA, 1900 - THE ARTISTS' PERSPECTIVE

first published 2000

by Greenhill Books, Lionel Leventhal Limited,
Park House, 1 Russell Gardens, London NW11 9NN
and
Stackpole Books, 5067 Ritter Road, Mechanicsburg, PA 17055, USA

British Library Cataloguing in Publication Data
Sharf, Frederic A.
The Boxer Rebellion : China 1900 : The Artists' Perspective
1.China - History - Boxer Rebellion, 1899-1901 - Pictorial works - Exhibitions
I.Title II.Harrington, Peter, 1954-
951'.035'0222

ISBN 1-85367-409-5

Library of Congress Catalog Card Number 00-021965

Designed by: Janell Lukac

Printed and bound in the United States of America
by Newburyport Press, Inc.

TABLE OF CONTENTS

ACKNOWLEDGEMENTS

This exhibition owes a great deal to the inspiration of my collaborator Peter Harrington,
Curator of the Anne S. K. Brown Military Collection, Brown University, Providence, Rhode Island.
Many years ago, Peter had the vision to recognize a collecting opportunity, and an exhibition potential.

The opening of the exhibition coincides with the publication in London of
China 1900, The Eyewitnesses Speak by Frederic A. Sharf and Peter Harrington (Greenhill Books).
Peter and I owe a large debt of gratitude to Lionel Leventhal and Kate Ryle of Greenhill
for their faith in this project, and for their willingness to make possible the publication
of an exhibition catalogue which incorporates some of the material from the book.

No exhibition can take place without a suitable venue, and we are very grateful to
Gene Schott, Director of the Heritage Plantation in Sandwich, Massachusetts
for providing such a location. In addition we are fortunate to have enthusiastic support
from Timothy Walch, Director, and Christine Mouw, Assistant Curator,
at the Herbert Hoover Presidential Library, West Branch, Iowa
which will provide the second and final location.

I am indebted to a handful of people who helped me to acquire the original
illustration artwork which makes up the bulk of this exhibition:

Glenn Mitchell and Jim Clancey, Maggs Brothers Ltd., London
Brian J. Newbury, Parker Gallery, London
Roger and Walt Reed, Illustration House, New York City
Richard Kossow, London
Eiko Ono, The Japanese Gallery, London
Christer von der Burg, Han-Shan Tang, London

Conservation of the artwork has been skillfully handled by Susan Duhl of Bala Cynwyd, Pennsylvania.
Matting and framing have been equally well carried out by Sande Webster and Mark Wallison
of the Sande Webster Gallery in Philadelphia.

Photography of all artwork was carefully executed by Mr. Chester Brummel,
Museum of Fine Arts, Boston, Massachusetts

I have been fortunate to have had the research assistance of William T. LaMoy,
Director of the James Duncan Phillips Library of the Peabody Essex Museum in
Salem, Massachusetts, and the cooperation of the staff of the Guildhall Library in London.
Research in Japan was conducted at the library of the Yokohama Archives, Yokohama,
where Hisako Ito of the Archives and Tom Okado of my own staff were of invaluable assistance.

The exhibition catalogue could not have happened without the editorial assistance and
organizational skills of my editor, Nancy TenBroeck of Salem, Massachusetts.

Lastly, I need to acknowledge the support of my wife, Jean,
who has encouraged me to pursue the material which made possible
the book, the exhibition, and the exhibition catalogue.

Frederic A. Sharf
Chestnut Hill, Massachusetts 02467, USA

2000

Heritage Plantation of Sandwich
67 Grove Street, Sandwich, MA 02563
May 13, 2000 - October 26, 2000

Herbert Hoover Presidential Library
210 Parkside Drive, West Branch, Iowa 52358
April 21, 2001 - October 28, 2001

INTRODUCTION TO THE EXHIBIT

The period known in history as the Boxer Rebellion is usually identified in the public mind with the fifty-five day siege of the Legation Compound in Peking, which started on 20 June 1900 and ended on 14 August. In reality, of course, a series of events began prior to the siege and continued to unfold well beyond the end of the actual siege.

World-wide attention was focused on the Far East in general, and on China in particular. Contemporary artists were required to look at a complex series of overlapping events and present these events to the public, which was hungry for images to accompany the newspaper reports. Many illustrations were produced, but relatively few survive; this exhibition presents a selection of these.

NORTH CHINA:
THE LOCATION OF THE CONFLICT

A traveler who wished to visit Peking in 1900 would arrive off the coast of China at the open roadstead of the Gulf of Pechihli, where all ocean-going ships were required to anchor. Passengers transferred to lighters and small steamships ten miles out to sea; conditions were normally turbulent, and often made more so by poor weather and high winds. It took about two hours to reach the Peiho River.

Only small ships could cross the sandbar at the mouth of the Peiho, after which they would find the Chinese city of Taku on the south bank of the river, and the western city of Tongku on the north bank. All passengers disembarked at Tongku, from which the railroad ran to Tientsin, a distance of approximately 30 miles, in two hours. Arriving at the Tientsin terminus, the Western traveler would need to cross to the south bank of the Peiho River to reach the Foreign Concession, which was totally separate from the enormous walled Chinese city of Tientsin.

Tientsin was an important commercial center, well situated at the junction of the Peiho River with the Grand Canal. (Before the opening of the railroad in 1897 there was enormous traffic to Peking on the river as far as Tungchow, and then over a stone paved road fifteen miles to Peking.) The Foreign Concession was mainly composed of three distinct western communities at this time: British, French, and German. The Japanese were just starting to construct their own community. Here were handsome buildings, excellent roads, gas lights, parks, churches, clubs, theaters—in short, an up-to-date, even elegant Western community totally separated from that of their Chinese neighbors.

From Tientsin the railroad continued to Peking, a distance of about 80 miles, requiring five hours. Its route was via Langfang and Fengtai to the Peking terminus at Machiapu, a few miles outside the walls of the Chinese City, a huge oblong-shaped walled city. Within the Tartar City was the Imperial City, which contained government offices, and the Forbidden City, with the royal palaces.

Adjacent to the Imperial City was the Legation Quarter, in which all foreign legations were located—each in its own walled compound. Each of the numerous Western missionary societies had walled compounds, but they were spread throughout the Tartar City, often at some distance from the Legation Quarter.

Most western visitors to Peking at this time found the city very unattractive. They complained especially about the crowded conditions, lack of proper sanitation, and unusual smells; the streets of Peking seemed overwhelmingly dirty. However, foreigners living within the Legation Quarter were

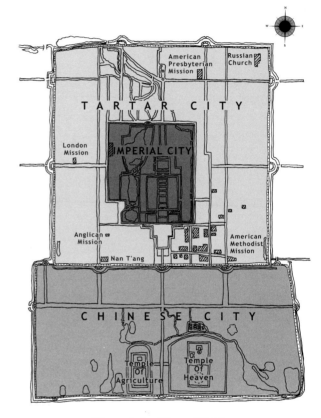

Plan of the City of Peking

housed in western style, with proper sanitation, and enjoyed a totally separate social life—dinner parties, dances, theatricals, picnics in the countryside, and their own horse racing track.

The Chinese populations of Tientsin and Peking were estimated at approximately one million each, though there was no scientific basis for the calculation. By contrast, the foreign populations of each city were minute—perhaps 500 in Peking and twice that in Tientsin. In each city, roughly half of the foreign population consisted of missionaries. In Peking the balance were primarily members of the diplomatic community, while in Tientsin most of the remainder were businessmen and their families.

HISTORICAL INTRODUCTION

It is necessary to place the confrontation which took place in the summer of 1900 between China and the Allies within a larger historical context. Thus, it is useful to think in terms of a ten-year period between the end of the Sino-Japan War in May 1895 and the end of the Russo-Japan War in September 1905. During these ten years the political situation in the Far

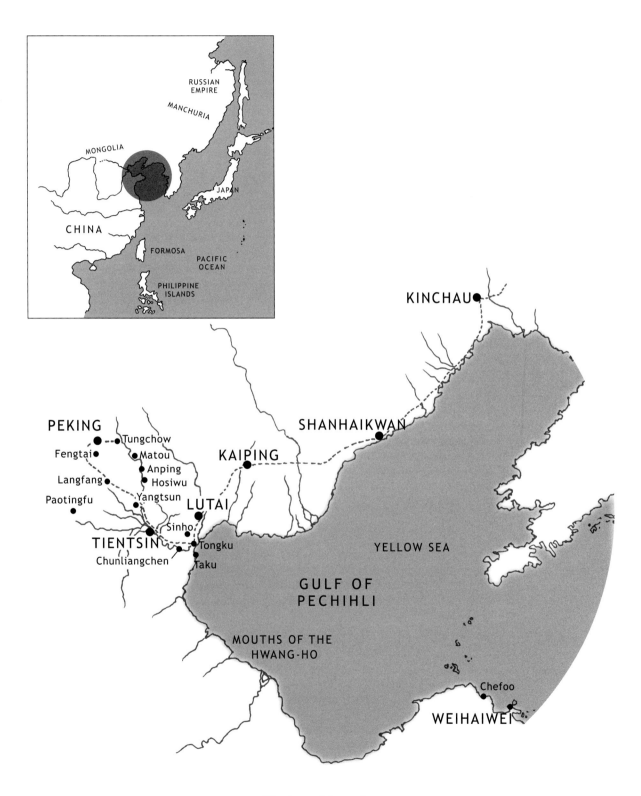

RUSSIAN
EMPIRE

MANCHURIA

MONGOLIA

JAPAN

CHINA

FORMOSA

PACIFIC
OCEAN

PHILIPPINE
ISLANDS

KINCHAU

PEKING
Tungchow
Fengtai
Matou
Anping
Langfang
Hosiwu
Paotingfu
Yangtsun
Sinho
TIENTSIN
Chunliangchen
Tongku
Taku

SHANHAIKWAN

KAIPING

LUTAI

YELLOW SEA

GULF OF
PECHIHLI

MOUTHS OF THE
HWANG-HO

Chefoo

WEIHAIWEI

The Area of Operations

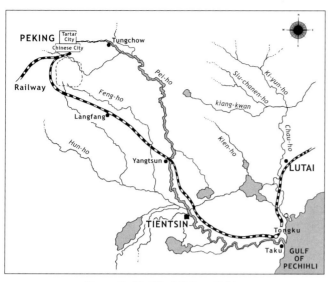

From Gulf of Pechihli to Peking

East changed. Japan became a major world power; Korea and Manchuria became important targets for economic exploitation; China was coming apart.

China's defeat by Japan in 1895 created an unstable environment within China. The Western powers at once began to seek concessions for mining rights and rights to construct railroads; then they seized territorial concessions. This increased Western presence within the Chinese Empire was the cause of anxiety among many Chinese, and ultimately led to dislike and distrust of all foreigners.

The Boxer movement was a logical outgrowth of this unrest and grew out of the drought, famine, and chronic unemployment in the North China provinces of Shantung and Chihli. The Boxer leaders created a peasant-based secret society committed to expelling foreigners from China.

The Boxers were a dangerous enemy. Colorful clothing and exotic ceremonies turned converts to the Boxer cause into fanatics who believed that they were invested with supernatural powers of invulnerability. Their Chinese name (*I Ho Ch'uan*) was translated into English as "Fists of Righteous Harmony"— an allusion to the strength which could come from a united effort.

The word "Boxer" first appeared in official Western correspondence in May 1898; by January 1900 the entire Western community in China was concerned, if not terrified. Boxer placards in towns and villages across North China proclaimed the motto: "Protect the Empire: Exterminate Foreigners." Because the anti-foreign message was also implicitly anti-Christian, the missionaries in the interior cities, as well as their Chinese converts, were the first targets and the first victims. Missionaries called for action to combat the Boxer threat; but diplomats and businessmen at first tended to regard the missionaries as crybabies.

The brutal murder of an Anglican missionary in Shantung Province on 31 December 1899 signalled an aggressive expansion of the Boxer cause. The movement spread from Shantung into Chihli; by the spring of 1900 the Boxers were active on the outskirts of Tientsin and Peking. Tungchow, only 13 miles from the walls of Peking, became a center for Boxer drills, attracting students and bargemen.

On 20 May 1900 Sir Robert Hart, the Inspector General of the Chinese Maritime Customs Service, wrote from his desk in Peking to his colleagues in London: "The Boxers are busy and mischief is intended. If my wife and children were here I'd move them off sharp to Japan."

On 28 May 1900 the Boxers destroyed the important railroad station at Fengtai, six miles from Peking, the junction for trains both to Peking and to Paotingfu. The British Legation, now sensing the gravity of the situation, notified British subjects in outlying communities that they could seek asylum within the Legation compound if they felt threatened.

THE SEYMOUR EXPEDITION

As the crisis in Peking deepened during the first week of June 1900, the various ministers at the legations in Peking began to communicate a sense of urgency to their home offices. An Allied fleet had assembled in the Gulf of Pechihli and on 9 June senior naval officers from many nations held a council of war aboard H.M.S. *Centurion*, the British flagship of Admiral Sir Edward Seymour. A decision was made to send a naval brigade to Peking under Seymour's personal direction. The Seymour Expedition, consisting of sailors and marines from all Allied ships, was assembled in a few hours. Early on the Sunday morning of 10 June, the men selected for this force were transferred from warships lying in the Gulf of Pechihli to small steam launches that could cross the bar at the entrance to the Peiho River and land at Tongku. They went at once by train to Tientsin.

The Seymour Expedition consisted of 2072 men, of whom 921 were British; Germany contributed 450; Russia 305; France 158; United States 112; Japan 54; Italy 40; and Austria 25. At Tientsin, five engines and more than 100 railroad cars were ready to take them to Peking. However, they had to turn back because the Boxers had torn up the rail tracks and because Seymour's men found themselves fighting not only Boxers, but also troops from the Chinese army who had joined the Boxers. Seymour was fortunate to be able to bring his men back to Tientsin two weeks later.

Admiral Seymour and staff

THE TAKU FORTS

The commanders of the Allied fleet, unaware of Seymour's problems, decided that it was important to take control of the group of Chinese forts located on the Gulf of Pechihli at Taku. Two forts were located on the north bank of the Peiho River and three on the south bank. The troops that occupied these forts were seen as a potential menace to Allied troops now arriving in China. On 16 June the Allied commanders ordered the Chinese to peacefully surrender control of all the forts on or before 2 AM on 17 June, or the Allies would occupy them by force.

Quite unexpectedly the Chinese initiated the confrontation, opening fire on the Allies at 12:50 a.m. on 17 June. The Allies landed a total force of 904 soldiers and sailors, of which 321 were British and 244 Japanese. Russia sent 159, Italy 25, and Austria 22; no Americans were permitted to participate by order of their commander. By 5 a.m. the Allies had seized the forts on the north bank, and by 7:10 a.m. the forts on the south bank were occupied and all action ceased.

THE SIEGE OF TIENTSIN

By this time, it was clear to the Chinese that the Allies intended to mount a massive military campaign against the Boxers. No sooner had Seymour departed on 10 June with his Relief Expedition than Allied troops and equipment began to arrive at Tientsin. The strategic location of this city, combined with the large concentration of Western businessmen and missionaries who resided there, meant that control of the city was vital for Chinese and for Westerners.

The Boxers (who by this time were cooperating with the Chinese Imperial soldiers under General Nieh) took action: on 15 June the telegraph wire between Tientsin and Taku was cut, thus isolating the residents from the outside world; on 17 June bombardments by the Chinese of the Foreign Concession commenced, initiating a 27-day siege. While not totally cut off as were their counterparts in Peking, the Western residents of Tientsin faced an uncomfortable and hazardous time.

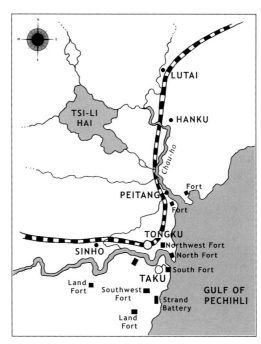

Taku Forts

On 23 June a relief force of Allied sailors, marines and soldiers reached Tientsin; on 24 June a large group of Russian soldiers arrived; and Seymour's troops returned on 25 June. Early in July American troops arrived from the Philippines and the Japanese 5th Army Division arrived from their base at Hiroshima. By 13 July the Allies had sufficient strength to initiate an attack on the Chinese Walled City, which was taken on the morning of 14 July. The Allies had now secured their base at Tientsin.

Barricade of sacks of rice near Emens residence, Tientsin, China, June, 1900
Courtesy, Peabody Essex Museum, Salem, MA

THE SIEGE OF PEKING

The Allied leaders in Peking, commanded by the British Minister Plenipotentiary, Sir Claude MacDonald, had on 20 June determined that the safest place for all foreigners was the British Legation compound. It was spacious, and had numerous buildings to house people and plenty of well water; it was surrounded by defensible walls. By the end of that day approximately 900 people were residing in a space meant for 60 people!

The actual area to be defended was, of course, much larger than simply the British Legation compound, as it encompassed much of the Foreign Legation section of Peking. There were 415 marine guards available from the eight countries that maintained legations in Peking, plus another 100 armed volunteers, some of whom had prior military experience.

The balance of the population consisted of men unwilling or unable to bear arms, plus women and children. MacDonald divided the remaining adults into various teams, each with responsibility for supervising numerous civilian needs—food, water, sanitation, medical.

When the siege ended, 66 people had died; of these, six were infants who died from malnutrition and the balance were men killed in the actual defense of the compound. No women died.

Admiral Seymour's failure to reach Peking in June, and the subsequent sieges at Tientsin and Peking, forced the Allies to mount a concerted effort to deal with the Boxers. British troops from India could reach China in less than 30 days, but Germany had to dispatch their troops from Europe, which often took 60 days. American troops from the Philippines arrived quickly, as did the Japanese troops from Hiroshima. Russia's base at Port Arthur enabled speedy supply of men. By the end of July a critical mass of Allied soldiers was assembled at Tientsin.

The Allies determined that the Expedition to relieve Peking would be commanded by Sir Alfred Gaselee, a British general with experience fighting on the North-West Frontier of India. He arrived at Tientsin on 27 July 1900 and departed for Peking on 4 August. He commanded approximately 20,000 troops, of whom half were Japanese. Russia contributed 4000; England 3000; United States 2000; France 800; Germany and Italy 200 each; Austria and Italy 50 each.

THE ALLIED RELIEF EXPEDITION

Departing from Tientsin on Saturday 4 August, they finally reached Peking on the morning of 14 August and quickly liberated the Legation Quarter. They found a city which was devastated and largely abandoned by its Chinese population. Shops were closed; streets were deserted; dead bodies were everywhere—many Chinese had been killed by their own Boxer countrymen.

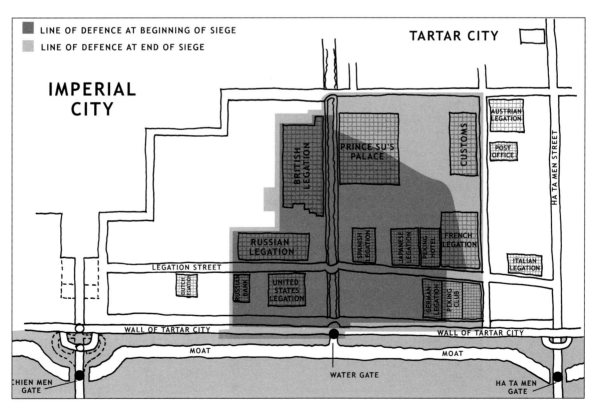

Legation Quarter

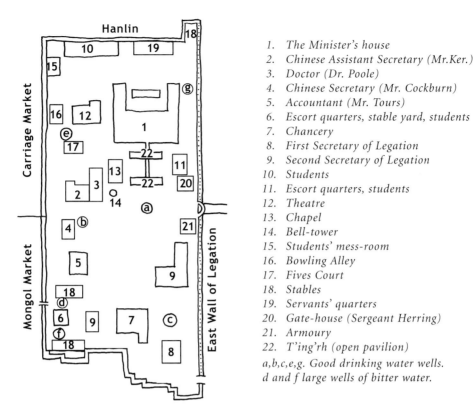

1. The Minister's house
2. Chinese Assistant Secretary (Mr.Ker.)
3. Doctor (Dr. Poole)
4. Chinese Secretary (Mr. Cockburn)
5. Accountant (Mr. Tours)
6. Escort quarters, stable yard, students
7. Chancery
8. First Secretary of Legation
9. Second Secretary of Legation
10. Students
11. Escort quarters, students
12. Theatre
13. Chapel
14. Bell-tower
15. Students' mess-room
16. Bowling Alley
17. Fives Court
18. Stables
19. Servants' quarters
20. Gate-house (Sergeant Herring)
21. Armoury
22. T'ing'rh (open pavilion)

a,b,c,e,g. Good drinking water wells.
d and f large wells of bitter water.

The Legation Compound

British Legation after the siege: student interpreters house
Photo by C.A. Killie

THE ALLIED OCCUPATION OF PEKING

The Allied occupation of Peking was an ambitious and complicated administrative process. The city was divided into zones of occupation, each under the control of one of the eight Allied nations.

The Boxers had discarded their exotic clothing, which meant that to the Allied soldiers any Chinese person might well be a hated Boxer. Under such circumstances, the Allied soldiers took out their desire for vengeance on anyone. With houses and shops abandoned, it is not surprising to find that the troops embarked on a prolonged looting campaign. Looting was prevalent not only among the soldiers but even more so among the Westerners who had endured the siege, with diplomats being among the worst offenders!

Meanwhile, there was an enormous influx of Allied soldiers. By September, the American troops numbered approximately 5,000, while Britain and Germany had 20,000 each. Ultimately the total of troops garrisoned in North China would reach almost 70,000—the largest foreign presence ever witnessed by the Chinese.

The Allies had decided to make the German General Count Alfred von Waldersee the Supreme Commander of all Allied troops in Peking. He had been sent to China by the Kaiser with specific instructions to avenge the murder of Minister von Kettler in June.

At this time the Allied troops in general and the German troops in particular embarked on a series of punitive expeditions designed to eradicate any and all pockets of Boxer sympathizers. Most of the men who participated in these expeditions had arrived too late to see action in July and August and they thirsted for action—and in the case of the Germans, for revenge.

AFTER 1901

With the signing of a Peace Protocol on 7 September 1901 the Allied forces in China were reduced to small units assigned to each of the Legations. However, it would be foolish to assume that peace returned to China. The Russians were seeking a larger presence in Manchuria; the Germans were establishing a major presence on the Shantung Peninsula; all Allied nations vastly increased their naval presence on what was known as the China Station.

Within a few years it was obvious to all nations that Japan and Russia would ultimately go to war over domination of Korea and Manchuria. Throughout 1903 war was expected; newspapers sent war correspondents; but no war was declared until February 1904. The world was amazed and shocked at Japan's success—an Oriental power had defeated a Western power for the first time.

When this war ended in September 1905 there was another huge burst of economic development in China. So the story of the Boxer Rebellion is only one chapter in a much longer and more complicated story of the conflict between China and the western world.

British Legation compound during the siege
Photo by C.A. Killie

House of secretary Henry Cockburn, secretary of the British Legation. Elegant house barricaded

CHRONOLOGY

CHRONOLOGY

1895

May: Treaty of Shimonoseki ratified, officially ending the Sino-Japan War 10 May
China is obligated to pay Japan a substantial indemnity

1896 Japan embarks on a ten-year program of naval expansion, with
the objective of building a new and modern fleet.
Russia obtains concession of land from China, to construct Siberian railway
through Manchuria

1897 Russia begins construction of a railway through Manchuria
November: Germans occupy Bay of Kiaochau on Shantung Peninsula

1898

March: Germans lease territory surrounding Bay of Kiaochau and start construction
of the European city of Tsingtau
Russians lease southern section of Liaotung Peninsula, including Port Arthur,
and start construction of European city of Dalny

April: French lease territory of Kwangchauwan around the Bay of Kwangchau

May: British flag raised at Weihaiwei to signify British lease of territory and harbor

July: British lease at Weihaiwei commences on 1 July

August: United States annexation of Hawaii and occupation of Philippine Islands

1899

February: United States annexation of Philippine Islands

September: United States Secretary of State, John Hay, proclaims in a series of notes the
"Open Door" policy which would entitle all nations equal trading rights
within China

December: Reverend Sidney Brooks, an Anglican missionary, is murdered
in Shantung Province by Boxers on 31 December

1900

May 30: Allied fleet begins to assemble outside Taku Bar in Gulf of Pechihli
Allied marines and sailors arrive at Tongku and Tientsin

May 31: Allied marines and sailors arrive at Peking Legations

June 5: Railroad service from Peking to Tientsin ceased

June 9: Peking Race Course destroyed by Boxers
Sir Claude MacDonald wires Admiral Seymour to send troops

June 10:	Telegraph line from Peking destroyed by Boxers Seymour Expedition departs from Tientsin
June 11:	Sugiyama Akira, Chancellor of the Japanese Legation, murdered in Peking
June 17:	Allied troops capture Taku Forts following bombardment Foreign Concession of Tientsin besieged by Boxers
June 19:	Tsungli Yamen demands all foreigners leave Peking
June 20:	Baron Klemens von Ketteler, German Minister, murdered in Peking Legation Quarter of Peking besieged Roman Catholic Mission at Peitang Cathedral besieged
June 23:	Allied Relief Column enters Tientsin
June 26:	Seymour Expedition returns to Tientsin
July 13:	Allied Army attacks Chinese Walled City, Tientsin
July 14:	Allied Army captures Chinese Walled City, Tientsin
July 17:	Truce at Legation Quarter in Peking
July 25:	Firing resumes in Peking for a few days
August 4:	Truce ends at Legation Quarter with resumption of heavy firing in evening Allied Relief Expedition departs Tientsin for Peking
August 5:	Allied victory at Peitsang
August 6:	Allied victory at Yangtsun
August 9:	Allied victory at Hosiwu
August 12:	Allied occupation of Tungchow
August 14:	Allied entry to Peking; relief of Legation Quarter
August 15:	Dowager Empress flees from Peking; Allied capture of Imperial City
August 16:	Allies capture Peitang Cathedral
August 28:	Allied victory parade in Forbidden City
September 3:	Prince Ching returns to Peking
September 8:	Punitive Expedition departs for Tiu-Liu

September 10:	Punitive Expedition departs for Liang-hsian
September 16:	Punitive Expedition departs for Pa-ta-chal
September 25:	Punitive Expedition departs for Nam-Hung-Men Field Marshall Alfred von Waldersee arrives at Taku
October 2:	Allied troops occupy Shanhaikwan Forts
October 3:	Troop review in Peking to honor departing Americans
October 10:	British troops occupy Summer Palace German troops occupy Winter Palace
October 12:	Punitive Expedition departs for Paotingfu
October 17:	Field Marshall von Waldersee arrives at Peking
October 20:	Allied occupation of Paotingfu. Sir Ernest Satow, British Minister Plenipotentiary, arrives in Peking to replace Sir Claude MacDonald
October 25:	Sir Claude MacDonald departs Peking for new posting at Tokyo
October 26:	Dowager Empress arrives at Sian (Xian)
November 6:	Return of Paotingfu Punitive Expedition
November 10:	First coating of ice on Peiho River at Tungchow; river traffic continues
November 12:	Punitive Expedition departs for Kalgan
December 7:	Peiho River frozen over, closed to traffic
December 9:	Train service from Tientsin to Peking resumes
December 12:	Train service from Peking to Tientsin and to Tongku resumes
December 22:	Allied Ministers present peace proposal terms to China
December 31:	Public execution of von Ketteler's confessed murderer

1901

January 1:	Parade of Allied troops in Peking
January 24:	News of death of Queen Victoria reaches Peking
January 27:	Troop review in honor of German Emperor

February 2:	Funeral Service for Queen Victoria and parade of Allied troops in her honor
February 19:	Celebration of Chinese New Year
February 26:	Public execution of two prominent Boxer leaders
March 6:	Parade of New South Wales Naval Brigade prior to their departure from China
March 10:	Bodies of siege victims removed from British Legation compound for burial in the European Cemetery outside the city wall
March 12:	Crisis in Tientsin; dispute between British and Russian soldiers over a railroad siding
March 19:	British Marines arrive at Tientsin railroad siding to replace Sikh soldiers
March 22:	Tientsin railroad siding crisis resolved; all troops withdrawn
March 27:	China offers to pay huge indemnity to Allies
September 7:	Peace Protocol of Peking signed by China and Allies; official ending of Boxer Rebellion

1902

January:	Anglo-Japanese Alliance; Treaty signed in London

1904

February 8:	Japanese army lands at Chemulpo
February 10:	Japan officially declares war
February 18:	Russia declares war

1905

May 28:	Japanese Navy destroys Russian fleet at Battle of Tsushima
September:	Treaty of Portsmouth signed on 5 September, officially ending Russo-Japan War.

THE ARTISTS' PERSPECTIVE

The events of 1900 in China created an unusual opportunity for artists. Newspapers and magazines still relied on drawings to depict and interpret contemporary events. But while the managers of media organizations attempted to forecast the outbreak of meaningful events in far-off places, so that artists and reporters could be sent in advance, this was not always possible.

Events in China in June of 1900 erupted suddenly, although there had certainly been numerous prior signals that China was in a turbulent mood. Thus, the major media organizations were unable to get men to China in a timely manner. This was further complicated by the significant British resources devoted to coverage of the Boer War in South Africa and the interest of the American press in events unfolding on the Philippine Islands.

To properly understand the artistic production which was instigated by events in China, it is necessary to divide this production into two segments:

1. Some professional artists were actually in China to witness, and to draw or photograph, the events; others arrived after the main action had taken place.

2. Much of the published art work was prepared in studios in the various Western countries, and in Japan, by studio-based professional artists. In some cases army and navy personnel sketched or drew what they were observing, and found a ready market for such sketches in London or New York. Staff artists then developed these sketches into finished, publishable artwork.

PROFESSIONAL ARTISTS ON SITE:

Adamson & Landor

Sydney Adamson and Arnold Henry Savage Landor (the latter not represented in this exhibition) were two artists, each with journalistic credentials as well, who managed to get to China in time to witness all the action. Adamson was already in the Far East, covering the American troops in the Philippines; and Landor had the foresight to set out for China before the extent of the disaster was well known.

On 20 June 1900 Adamson was in Tarlac with the American army, when he was ordered by *Leslie's Magazine* to go to China. Fortunately his lengthy service in the Philippines had given him friends among the American army officers, and he was able to reach China on an American troop transport, the USST *Logan*, which proceeded to Nagasaki, arriving on 2 July for coaling. Adamson took advantage of the overnight stay in Nagasaki to interview the British crew of HMS *Whiting*, who had come from Taku to have their ship repaired.

Adamson reached Taku on 10 July, and Tientsin on 11 July. Thus he was able to accompany the American army on its first mission—the overthrow of the Chinese City of Tientsin on 13 and 14 July 1900. He then marched with the American army to Peking, witnessed the entry of the Allied armies into the city on 14 August, and stayed on through

the winter of 1901 to cover the occupation of Peking as well as the various punitive expeditions. His final reports from Peking were sent in February 1901, and by March he would have been able to travel from Peking by river to Tientsin, and to Taku.

Landor was born in Florence, Italy, on 2 June 1867, and was educated in Italy and in Paris as an artist. In 1888 he embarked on a trip around the world, supporting himself along the way by painting portraits of famous people. In 1893 he published his first book, dealing with experiences in Japan living among the Ainu peoples; subsequent books dealt with visits to Korea and to Tibet.

In 1899 he was in Nepal on a mountain-climbing trip. When he returned to England he sensed an opportunity to get to China before other journalists; he embarked in early June 1900, travelling by way of New York and reaching Vancouver in time to catch the 19 June sailing of the *Empress of Japan*. Thus he arrived in Yokohama on 2 July and pushed on at once for China, probably travelling to Shanghai and then up the coast to Taku in a small steamer. His drawings, as well as his own photographs, were used to illustrate his 1901 book entitled *China and the Allies*.

While Adamson and Landor reached the scene of battle in time, there were many intrepid correspondents who did not. We shall thus look at the odyssey of two men who tried but failed.

Whiting & Schonberg

In June 1900 England was consumed by the dire news emanating from China, but it was not until early in July that the magnitude of the disaster in Peking made it clear to the media in London that special coverage was needed. At the same time, the buildup of troops was apparent: Japanese, American, and German troops in substantial numbers were *en route* to China and it was evident that an important campaign was unfolding.

Fred Whiting and John Schonberg missed the real fighting through the conservatism of their respective employers. Whiting was working for *The Graphic* and Schonberg for *The Illustrated London News*. Each publication hesitated in sending a staff person until the news in China got so bad that journalistic integrity required the dispatch of their own correspondent. Whiting departed on 13 July, and Schonberg one week later.

At this time the experienced war correspondents were in short supply; most were in South Africa and some were seriously ill as a result of their experiences there. The proprietors of *The Graphic* needed a man who could both describe and illustrate events in China; and Fred Whiting was chosen for the assignment, probably on very short notice. He started out on Friday, 13 July 1900 and probably reached Shanghai on 13 August, when he found that it was impossible to proceed further north on any scheduled steamship. He took a cattle ship bound for Taku and reached Tientsin on Sunday, 19 August. He had missed the major military campaign and the story of the relief of Peking. However, he proceeded with a military convoy and reached Peking at the end of August.

Whiting remained in Peking until March 1901. He sent a large quantity of drawings and sketches back to London; after

2 months in transit, some of the drawings were reproduced as he had drawn them, while others were redrawn by studio artists in London.

We know less about the actual itinerary of John Schonberg, but can assemble a pretty good estimate from the various drawings reproduced in *The Illustrated London News* (not included in the exhibit). It is likely that he was a week behind Whiting. *The Illustrated London News* published the first of his drawings in August, from Suez *en route* to Hong Kong. By 25 August he was at Weihaiwei, where he sketched a scene in a British hospital; by the end of August he had reached Tientsin. His first group of China drawings was published on 27 October, approximately 60 days after he would have mailed them at Tongku.

Since it was not easy for correspondents to arrange transport to Peking, Schonberg remained a few days in Tientsin. He interviewed eyewitnesses; he explored the localities; he could thus supply the *News* with drawings of events which had already taken place. Then he went to Tungchow by junk with a British supply convoy, arriving there on 11 September and presumably reaching Peking the next day.

He quickly learned the ropes in Peking and was able to accompany the punitive expedition to Pa-Ta-Chou on 16 September—his first eyewitness account of actual military action.

MILITARY ARTISTS ON SITE

Numerous men of the Allied armies and navies were competent enough to sketch what they saw, or to take snapshots with their personal cameras. They recognized that the media in London and New York would pay handsomely for such eyewitness material; so they mailed it off and waited for their remittance.

The newspapers and magazines all had professional artists on staff to turn these submissions into finished artwork. Usually the man who had submitted the original sketch or photo is credited in the published account; but often his name is misspelled or his initials are given incorrectly, so it is often necessary to use some imagination when trying to find out who had taken the time to mail his observation from China.

In looking at the contribution of army officers to the artistic coverage of the Boxer Rebellion, one officer in particular stands out—Captain Francis Gordon Poole of the East Yorkshire Regiment. Poole was experienced in colonial warfare; he had served in Central Africa in 1897, and in Northern Rhodesia in 1898. He had joined the army in 1892 as a 2nd Lieutenant, and was still a young man. In 1899 he came to Peking to reside for one year with his brother and to study Chinese. (Captain Woodsworth Poole was the chief medical officer at the British Legation in Peking.)

Francis Gordon Poole was trapped in Peking in June 1900. He was assigned to command all volunteers within the besieged Legation Compound, and was attached to the British Marine Guard for that purpose. He was slightly wounded during the siege. He remained on in China after the end of the siege, serving with the China Field Force as Transport Officer and as Railway Staff Officer. He was mentioned in dispatches and received the Distinguished Service Order (DSO).

There is no way to know what prompted Poole to sketch his surroundings and to submit the sketches to *The Graphic* in London, but this was done by many British army officers.

Another artist whose work found its way into the pages of *The Graphic* was an ordinary sailor on HMS *Endymion* named Robert Barr. The *Japan Weekly Mail* of 17 November 1900 reported that: "It is interesting to note that two spirited full-page sketches in a recent number of The Graphic were contributed by Mr. Robert Barr, a blue-jacket of the *Endymion*, who was on Admiral Seymour's expedition. The sketches were of course paid for at a handsome rate."

Unfortunately much of the artistic production prompted by events in China in 1900 has long ago disappeared, but further study of any remaining material should certainly be considered.

PERSONAL OBSERVATIONS

SYDNEY ADAMSON IN CHINA:
SOME PERSONAL OBSERVATIONS

Peking, China, August 30th, 1900

The real finish of our march to Peking was a tea-party. In spite of an attempt to ignore the correspondents we all insisted upon being invited. It is true that we are "no class," and are not permitted to wear shoulder-straps and thingumijigs on our breasts, but nevertheless our united force did what the Chinese absolutely failed to do—brought the allied forces to terms....

I talked with Captain Hutchinson, of General Chaffee's staff, about permission to accompany the military march which was to take place with much pomp and circumstance on Tuesday, the 28th day of August 1900. When the captain had recovered his breath after the shock of hearing any mere civilian talk of entering this holy of holies, he proceeded to read me a lecture on the immense seriousness of the occasion. I failed to be properly impressed....I grew tired of the lecture and asked for a decision. This much overworked assistant adjutant-general said he would put it to the general if he had time, and again impressed upon me that General Chaffee was on the point of expiring from overwork....

I appealed to Major Lee, of the general's staff. The major is at all times a courteous gentleman, and he happens to be a friend. He spoke to the general, but by then the edict had gone forth. The correspondents were prohibited. The American czar had spoken. I received my letter, neatly folded, and on the edge the polite and expressive intimation that it was "disapproved," followed by many flourishes and the invincible captain's name.

This was on the morning of the 27th; next day was the event. I had sent in a similar letter to the British general, on the principle that a double permission could do no harm, while one out of two might succeed. I was registered with the British forces as a correspondent, and happening to be a British subject I thought I would try my luck in that quarter. My letter was returned to me with the information that as an American citizen I should apply to General Chaffee. I saw Captain Phillips and put him right about the nationality. The captain told four of us that morning that no passes were to be issued then, and there was a vagueness about the replies to our further questions that settled the matter in our minds. We were to be refused.

We four formed a meeting then and there, roped in another correspondent riding through the British legation, and each agreed to inform one or two others, and all met in the bell-tower of the British Legation at two o'clock. Mr. O'Dowd had drawn up a protest, which we all signed, and Captain Phillips took it in to General Sir Alfred Gaselee....

Peking, August 27th

To General Sir Alfred Gaselee. Sir:—The undersigned special correspondents duly licensed to accompany the British forces, having been informed unofficially that they are not to be given proper facilities for witnessing and recording the triumphal entry of the troops into the palace tomor—row, beg to enter a strong protest. They would urge that their presence is in the highest degree necessary for the adequate description of so important an occasion, of the very deepest interest to the whole civilized world.

The correspondents have been sent here at considerable expense to represent and keep informed the people at home; they have shared in the dangers and discomforts of the campaign; and at the eleventh hour to arbitrarily withdraw from them the privileges duly granted will not merely cast a slur upon them as representatives of the public, but cause deep and widespread disappointment at home.

We have the honor to be, sir, yours respectfully,

[Signed]   Joseph H. O'Dowd, *Daily Mail*, London
George Lynch, *Daily Express* and *The Sphere*, London
T. Cowen, *Daily News* and *The Standard*, London
Frank Geere, *Reuters*, London
Sydney Adamson, *Leslie's Weekly* and *Evening Post*, New York
F. W. Eddy, *Associated Press*
W. J. Hernon, *New York Journal* and German papers.

....In the evening our permission was given us with the air of a gift to naughty children, and we were all sent home after many grave requests to be good and not to break ranks and not to loot. We then heard that General Chaffee had relented, and American papers could go in. Geere was still prohibited, but he came just the same. After the march was over, and we were all wandering around looking at things and drinking tea, handed out by real blue-button mandarins, the only people who were too busy with pencil and camera not to touch and chip pieces off as souvenirs were the correspondents....

Peking, September 7th, 1900

The 28th day of August, 1900, by some of us, will be marked by a white stone. It was the day set aside for the official opening of China's most secret recesses. It will not be the less appreciated by the correspondents, as they had to fight for admission; but that is a story already told. The morning broke clear and sunny, but as the day advanced the clouds, soft and gray as down, crept over the sky and prevented the glare and the heat. The British troops were forming in a compound north of their legation when I arrived to find my place in the column. The British officers kept up their reputation as the cleanest, smartest, and best-horsed of all the troops. In point of cleanliness in clothing and accoutrements, and in general bearing, the "Tommies" and the Indian troops were an easy first. When the Russian column filed through to the swing of a martial air we were all surprised to see that they were moderately clean. Then some of the Japs followed, headed by the general and staff. They were all smart and well uniformed.

The Japanese officers wore black frogged jackets, spotless white trousers, and glazed black riding-boots. Add to this a colored band round the cap, with gold star, white gloves, and all the bright metals glistening on swords, spurs, and buckles, with handsome saddle leathers and well-groomed mounts, and you have a turn-out that resembles the military millinery of a European parade-day. The Russians' baggy trousers, worn by blousy, ill-set-up officers, will never appeal to me as smart.

All this, however, was only a glimpse behind the scenes just before the performers gain the stage. Through one of these everlasting gates that face one on every hand in Peking the British column filed and halted, drawn up with its left resting on the central walk that leads through three more gates, and then within the palace grounds. The Russian general, a fine-looking old fellow, inspected the lines and paid many compliments to the Britishers. I wondered what he really thought, for these are some of the men he will have to fight—some day. It is interesting to note, while passing, just what the Indian troops themselves think. They had heard much about the Russian as the one great enemy to be tackled when the big fight comes, but they had not seen him till they landed in China. They have come to the same conclusion as the American soldier, that the Russian isn't much good, and they are ready to take him on any day. When they first saw the Americans they said to their English officers: "Why, these are our own people, and yet—not quite the same."

Twenty-one guns were fired by a battery of the Royal Horse Artillery as the Russians, leading the column, marched on through the palace gates. The march began at eight o'clock. Next to the Russians came the Japanese, then the British, and following them the Americans. Then came the Germans, the French, the Austrians, and Italians. On entering the gate under the huge palace that sits on the wall, the first court of the sacred city opens before one. Straight across the court-yard is another gate within a building which is really a pillared hall. This hallway, paved with stone and raised by a flight of steps above the court-yard, runs round three sides of the inclosure. To the right and to the left of the central gates are two smaller gates, and on the eastern and western ends are two others that lead into courts on the right and left. The whole court-yard is paved with rough, heavy stones intergrown with weeds that seem to have known no hindrance for years.

Across the court-yard from east to west runs a moat or ornamental waterway, with sides of well-cut stone. This piece of water curves at each end, like a Chinese bow. It is crossed by five marble bridges, and on the flagstones are carved dragons. The water is stagnant and covered with a heavy layer of green scum, only broken by the bloated, blue mass of a dead Chinaman. Just within the gates are two peculiarly formed pillars, beautifully carved in low relief with the imperial dragon. In front of the marble steps that lead to the first gate are two large green griffins. The character of this sculpture and the fine workmanship win for it a high place in art of its kind. The beams of all these buildings are of heavy wood, well-formed and employed in a manner most enduring and effective. All the ceilings and beams are painted or lacquered in brilliant but harmonious colorings....

The most inspiring moment of the whole day was the military ceremony at the end of the march. The Russians lined up in three double ranks on each side of the line of march, with the band on the left, as the column marched near the final gateway. As the colors of the various forces passed, national airs were played and the marching troops presented arms. Groups of officers formed around the gateway and cheered with the rest. The Japanese troops were lined up just outside the gate....

....It was the great show-day—the parade of victorious troops through the heart of the enemy's country. When the Russians came through, with their rolling gait, singing that strange chant that is filled with the sound of bells, they swung past the Japanese without looking to note their faces. But every Japanese, from the generals to the privates, watched every Russian with a serious, critical look; every man was a possible enemy, and with shut mouths they took their measure. It might be a big job, but the Japs are not afraid.

When all the troops had gone the generals and staff officers, the ministers and secretaries, accompanied by some ladies and the correspondents, started back through the grounds. Under some old trees that are dead, but held in position by beams and iron, mandarins and palace attendants served tea and candied fruits and nuts to the victors. Those old trees never before cast their shadows on so strange a scene. The old rooks flew from tree to tree and told each other of the wonderful things happening below. Some of the mandarins are fine-looking men, but their costumes are so theatrical, and their figures so old-womanish that I am always struck with an apparent lack of manliness and force. They look dreamy and serious. A heavy, lethargic gravity seems to envelop them. Their faces and manner indicate a certain culture, but they appear sluggish and unhealthy, devoid of life and fire, lacking in any of those forces that impel a race onward and give it the power to grapple with others and hold its own....

FRED WHITING IN CHINA:
SOME PERSONAL OBSERVATIONS

ON THE WAY TO PEKING

[Tsingtau–August 15, 1900]

I left the S.S. *Chusan* at Shanghai, where I found I should have to wait several days for a steamer proceeding north to Taku. Shanghai, or, rather, the European Settlement, is a beautiful city, with big white stone buildings and avenues of trees. Under the shade of the trees along the river front are hundreds of rickshaws, drawn by sturdy Chinese coolies, waiting to be hired—so many that one cannot help wondering how they all make a living, especially as for the sum of five cents (about 1 1/4 d.) one can travel a distance fully equal to a shilling cab fare in London. The whole city has an appearance of wealth, and on an autumn evening in the gardens, with a band playing, and well-dressed people everywhere, it might be a favourite watering-place in England. The appearance of everybody dressed in white, and the loud buzz of insects, and native servants carrying chairs, bring one forcibly back to the East. Here I fell in with another special correspondent, and we decided to proceed to the front together. Our first idea was to get our ponies and stores, though we took as little as possible, in order to get along quickly. My new friend's knowledge of the Chinese was most useful to us, and we soon found ourselves in the stables of a well-known Shanghai dealer, where, after trying a number of the animals brought out for our inspection, we finally selected a couple of useful-looking nags, suitable for our purpose. They were sturdy little animals, brought down in droves every year from Mongolia. This year they have all been bought up by German agents for shipment to the north, so we had to pay about double what they were worth.

We were glad at last to find ourselves on board a German cattle-boat bound north, though our troubles soon began. Some of the cattle died on the way—which was not pleasant in this climate—and we also found that, instead of going right through, as is usual, we were to call at Tsingtau, where we were delayed something like thirty hours. Though very much annoyed by our delay, Tsingtau itself was interesting, and worth a visit, as showing how quickly the Germans, who came here about three years ago, are turning a small Chinese fishing village into a flourishing town. Already there are two big hotels, one named after Prince Henry, who was out here a year or two ago. Here we first noticed the Chinese wheelbarrow, made of wood—bearings included—which can be heard, like a giant cricket, about a mile away.

ON THE WAY TO PEKING: AT TIENTSIN

[Tientsin–August 20, 1900]

On arriving at Tientsin [19 August] we found the station—or what remains of it—one big camp for Russians, Germans, and Japs. There had been a fight that morning, when the 6th American Cavalry and Bombay Cavalry were engaged. During the engagement Lieutenant Gawsen saved the life of an American cavalryman under a concentrated fire. I went to the Guard-house and made a sketch of some of the prisoners, all of whom were Boxers, the Imperial troops having bolted as usual. Tientsin, which has, I should think, been a pretty town, is now an utter ruin. The streets are paraded by the tall, serious-looking Sikhs, the little Japs—who, by the way, every one is praising—and the English and German blue-jackets.

We found on inquiry at headquarters, where we procured our passports, that a convoy was starting the next morning for Peking, the first to leave since the relief. The convoys to Peking go either by road or river. We decided to go by road the first part of the journey, and catch the boats about two-thirds of the way there. Up at four the next morning, we found the 1st Coolie Corps, as it is named, with its escort of Madras Pioneers starting. This corps of 1,000 coolies was raised in five days by Captain Rose, 1st Ghoorkas [sic], and Lieutenant Alexander, 6th Bombay Cavalry, from the district of Lahore. It was the first time, I understand, that a coolie corps had left India for foreign service. A mode of transport suggested for these parts has been the Chinese wheelbarrow, and no doubt this would be an excellent means, but as it is an art to wheel one the Coolie Corps was supplied with small light Japanese carts, capable of carrying about 3 1/2 cwt. These have been found to answer well. The road, or rather track, lies through immense fields of millet, growing to a height of from twelve to fifteen feet. The track is in parts very bad indeed, and in wet weather absolutely impassable.

IN THE CELESTIAL CITY

[Peking–August 30, 1900]

At last [30 August] I have reached the Celestial City, though never was there a greater misnomer. It is the filthiest city on earth, and in ruins, with closed shops, from which a Chinese head is now and then protruded, but soon withdrawn. Mangy dogs prowl round the carcass of a horse, while instead of Chinese the soldiers of the allied forces patrol the streets.

Our journey to Peking was uneventful, though the country was in a very unsettled state. We were on several occasions fired at, and ranged our carts up in the form of a zareba; but no attack was made. The last part of the journey by river was a tedious business—nothing but shallows and sand banks to cross every few miles. The boats were towed by coolies stark naked. When a boat became stranded all the coolies would get into the water, and, chattering, laughing, and singing, would pull, push, and lever the boat off. The feature of the river, and indeed of all the villages on the line of march—which, by the way, were all deserted—was the number of dead bodies everywhere, chiefly Chinese, while the crops, probably the most magnificent crops in the world, were rotting for want of reapers. One of my sketches shows our boatmen at breakfast. I greatly delighted this man by presenting him with a ticket on which I had written "Boatman to the English convoy." This ticket he wore like a medal on his breast.

WITH THE ALLIES IN PEKING: DESTROYING A BOXER STRONGHOLD

[Peking–September 18, 1900]

I started out this week with Reuters correspondent [Frank Geere] on what promised to be an interesting expedition—the first in which the Allied Powers had worked together since the taking of Peking—the object being the destruction of a Boxer stronghold, Pa-ta-chal, the place of the eight temples, about twelve miles north-west of the city. As a rule, these expeditions are kept profoundly secret—why nobody seems to know—but on this occasion rumour was rife the day before. The force we accompanied was composed of British and Americans; other columns of Japanese, Germans, and Austrians left the city at different gates, each taking separate road to their respective positions, the object being to surprise and surround the enemy.

We left Peking at about five o'clock in the afternoon [16 September], the column having started two hours before. Soon after leaving by the north-west gate of the Chinese city we came upon striking evidence of the state of the stone roads of China (the famous roads laid down in the dim past ages of China's greatness) by an American transport cart sinking down to the hub in a gap between the stones. No sooner—after strenuous exertions—was it righted than it was in another place a bit worse. We saw the cart on its way and then pushed on, as it was getting dark and we had now left the stone road and were on the open country following the tracks of the column. These tracks, after a few miles, were not so easy to find to unpractised eyes, and on coming to a branch road—or rather track, as there are no real roads—we had to strike matches to find the newest wheel marks. At the first village we came to we knock up an old Chinaman, who appeared very much frightened, and made him water our horses while he put our *mafoo*, or groom, on the right road. As it was pitch dark we had to proceed very slowly, but about this point we could see the reflections of the bivouac fires against the sky, and were glad to reach Lui-ku-chau, where we cooked our supper and turned in for two hours' rest on the counter of a Chinese pawnshop.

The Advance on the Stronghold

We hardly seemed to have closed our eyes when we were awakened by the many sounds of a camp stirring and troops preparing to start. It was a cold, wet morning, and saddling up in the dark was not inspiring, with little prospect of breakfast. I came across a friend in an officer of the 26th Beluchistans, who made me have a cup of hot coffee and some sandwiches. We found the column in the grey of the morning trailing across the plains towards the distant hills—our objective—like an army of ghosts. No sound was heard but the squelching of the men's boots in the sodden ground.

After marching for an hour or so with our clothes wet through, a misty-looking sun appeared over the high *kowliang* [note: a crop like corn] and did something towards drying our clothes. We rode on past the column and joined the staff of General Wilson, of the American Army, who was in command. On reaching the head of the column a peculiar sight presented itself. A few scouts of the Bengal Lancers riding on ahead had rounded up a crowd of frightened villagers and, tying them together by their pigtails, brought them before the General, whereupon they all flopped on to their knees, kow-towing and prostrating themselves, as is their custom. The General, after a few minutes' conversation with an interpreter, ordered them all to be allowed to go free, to the seeming great surprise of the Indian soldiers in charge of them. The troops were here halted for a short time while the sappers cut a road for the artillery from the high fields in which we were marching to the road below.

A Wretched Resistance

The Sikhs and Americans now advanced on the hills about a mile in front of us, rising suddenly from the plain and overlooking the Boxer stronghold, while another company of the same troops executed a flanking movement to the right, advancing on the Boxer position by skirting the hills. The Japanese in the meantime had taken up a position threatening the rear of the enemy, who would have been completely surrounded had the Germans and Austrians come up in time, which, however, they failed to do. The road was thus left open for the retreat of the enemy, of which they were not slow to avail themselves. The few who were left in the town made a wretched resistance. The firing was short and sharp; now and then one could hear the Sikhs or Beluchis give a wild hill cry as they hit their man. After a very stiff climb, leading our ponies up the face of the hill, we descended in time to be with the troops when they entered the town. After the fight I examined some of the poor wretches who, with their one Gatling gun, old-fashioned rifles, and primitive swords and spears, thought they were a match for European troops. They all wore the Boxer uniform. This consists of a red turban, red sash, and anklets over the blue costume of the peasant, while in a pouch in the waistband each man carries a charm against bullets in the form of a paper slip covered with mystic characters. The wounded were very quickly attended to, and seemed grateful, although they bore the pain wonderfully. I wandered into one of the temples, and found everything indicating sudden flight, things being thrown about on the floors and the tea still in the cups in the priests' quarters. The temples were afterwards blown up as a sort of retaliation for wrecking the Summer Palaces. The troops then returned to Peking.

These expeditions are useful in keeping the country around Peking safe and free from the enemy, enabling the farmers to gather their crops and bring provisions to the city for sale.

[Peking–September 30, 1900]

When the International troops entered Peking, the city was looted by the men, but the British troops were not allowed to loot indiscriminately. All inhabited houses were respected, and so too was the property of all Chinese houses known to be friendly. The loot was put up to auction and the proceeds were given to the prize fund for soldiers. The auction sales are always crowded, people of all nationalities being present. [1]British officers are among the principal buyers. Though prices are fairly high, grand bargains are made sometimes.

A BRUSH WITH THE BOXERS:
WITH THE GERMAN EXPEDITION TO NAN-HUNG-MEN

[Peking–September 30, 1900]

The Germans have a quiet but businesslike way of doing things, and I was not surprised to hear one evening that early the following morning they were to start on a punitive expedition on a fairly large scale. The whole thing had been arranged in a few hours, on information brought in by Lieutenant Von Hoepfner, who, with a party of scouts numbering about twenty, was fired upon by the enemy from a temple near the Emperor's hunting park—a gigantic expanse of prairie enclosed by a wall about ten miles due south of Peking. That a large body of Boxers was in the neighbourhood was known, as a week previously the Japs had had a fight near the railway at a village called Huang-Tsun, proving that the country was by no means settled and safe for travelling. I got news late in the evening, and four o'clock the next morning found Reuters correspondent and myself outside the gates of the German Legation, as we had received special permission from the German General Von Hoepfner to accompany the force. Our mule-cart carried our kit and three days' provisions.

---

1. Editor's note: These auctions took place every afternoon except Sunday, under the colonnade in front of the British Legation. Sales were open to anyone, but the British officers predominated. The Russians and French never came; the Americans and Germans came infrequently. The Japanese, as well as employees of various Legations, were regular attendees.

Leaving Peking

It was not yet daylight [25 September], and in the gloom could be distinguished the General and staff, with their Chinese servants and ponies, and here and there a sturdy German orderly. We left the west gate of the Chinese city, this being the German quarter of Peking. The market people (who, by the bye, are already gaining confidence and returning) were busy arranging their wares. About a mile outside the city we found the German soldiers—heavy, sturdy-looking fellows—with their cumbersome kit, which, however, did not seem to affect their marching powers. The expedition consisted of two battalions of infantry, one battery of artillery, and a detachment of sappers. The column marched due south until it arrived at Huang-Tsun, where we crossed the railway and came upon a detachment of Japanese, who accompanied our column. Here we halted for breakfast. The villagers—or those of them who were not too afraid—did all they could by watering our horses and fetching grain. One of the things which struck me was the number of big piles of railway sleepers all about the village, brought in by the enemy after they had pulled up the railway. About five miles further south were covered, but without discovering any signs of the enemy, although a collection of arms in some of the houses showed that they had been occupied at a very recent date. The village was bare, and the troops then made a move in the direction of Nan-hung-men—a place known to be in possession of the Boxers. Our road now lay through large fields of kowliang, almost hiding the soldiers.

The Fight Among the Corn

It was getting late, and, evening coming on, we had quite given up the idea of meeting any of the Boxers when our scouts came galloping back. We were at the same time greeted by a regular fusillade from a clump of trees in the centre of the corn, while from the walls of the hunting park stretching away on our left came more firing. Our men now advanced, deploying through the high corn, while our artillery was brought into action, shelling the position from which the firing first started. I went forward with the troops, and was rewarded by coming upon an open space in the kowliang, where a curious sight presented itself. A party of about thirty Boxers, evidently headed off, were facing the Germans, and going through their dance, or Boxer movements. They were led by a man on a white horse. He wore, like most of these people, bright red sashes and shoulder belts, and a bright coloured cloth wound round his head. The Boxers were armed with Manlicher rifles, spears, and swords, but the whole of them in a short time were shot down, while four of our men were wounded. Each Boxer carries in a sort of pouch made of cloth–worn like a sporran—a charm, a piece of paper on which are written in blood Chinese characters, which the poor fellow thinks will render him impervious to the bullets of the foreigner. He also holds the belief that if a man is killed by foreign soldiers he will come to life again in seven days. After the fight we camped for the night in the village, the general and staff selecting the Temple to sleep in. Being pitch dark, and cold, we were glad, after some trouble in getting wood, to cook our supper and turn in. Seeing a blaze, I went to find out what it was, and saw the soldiers throwing the idols of the joss-house into a big fire, to make room for their quarters for the night.

THE AMERICANS AT PEKING

[Peking–October 7, 1900]

Generals Wilson and Chaffee reviewed the entire American force at Peking [3 October], previously to the departure of those who were returning. The review took place on the wide expanse of ground between the Temple of Heaven and the Temple of Agriculture, the same ground having been occupied as a camp by the Chinese General Tung-fu-hsiang before the taking of Peking by the allies. It was a real Peking day, with a hot and clear sky, but clouds of blinding dust. Everybody in Peking turned out to do honour to the Americans, who looked extremely workman-like in their khaki, while some wore blue jerseys. The men gained the highest praise from the military critics for their admirably executed march past.

PUNISHING THE BOXERS:
WITH THE PAOTINGFU EXPEDITION [1]

[Tientsin–November 6, 1900]

There had been rumours for many weeks beforehand of a big expedition to Paotingfu, the capital of the province and a noted anti-foreign city, which was practically the centre of the Boxer movement. The object of the expedition was the punishment of towns and villages and the degradation of the chief inhabitants of the district concerned in the rising. The departure of the troops had been delayed by the

Germans, who, in spite of their name for organisation, were very deficient in transport. This they started to remedy by seizing any carts or mules not actually belonging to other Powers, giving a note to the owner to the effect that he could claim the animals again after the expedition. So, on arriving home one night, I was not surprised to hear my *mafoo*, or groom, with a melancholy look, inform me that the Germans had taken my mule. I went round at once to the German headquarters, and, after a lot of trouble, got my animal back. A column, under General Gaselee, left Peking, consisting of British, Germans, French, and Italians, while a larger column left Tientsin and joined ours at Paotingfu.

No Fighting

I accompanied the Peking column and returned with the Tientsin column, through the kindness of the officers of the 3rd Bombay Cavalry, who invited me to their mess. I had thus a good opportunity of seeing the whole Boxer country. The march to Paoting was altogether uneventful. Those who fondly imagined that we should have fighting with the Imperial Chinese troops discovered that, in obedience to the orders of Li-Hung-Chang, they had evacuated all the big towns on our line of march and taken up positions some ten miles away on either flank, allowing us, as the Chinese put it, a free passage. The country here is absolutely flat as far as the eye can reach, but is relieved by clumps of trees overshadowing villages, most of which are protected by a moat and mud wall. In many cases we found well-constructed trenches and streets barricaded and loopholed, but the Boxer we did not find. Instead, the villagers met us with pails of water for our horses and offers of fowls and eggs.

THE TRICOLOUR EVERYWHERE

[October 14th]

At the first walled town we came to, Lo-li-ho, we found that a column of French cavalry, which appears to have acted quite independently of the other troops, had already preceded us, the tricolour floating over the gate and a notice stating that the town was "Sous la protection de la France." This, with the hundreds of small flags everywhere, caused a certain amount of wrath in a neighbouring nation, until it was discovered that the Chinese had been quick to imitate the flag themselves, and every village we passed through afterwards had the tricolour over each door.

A Haul for the Germans

The British were the only troops who carried tents and encamped every night, the others billeting in the villages and towns. At one of these towns—An-hsu—the Germans, who were for that day [17 October] in rear of the column, took out a party of fifty mounted men to a distance of ten miles or so, ostensibly to get forage, though the town, like all the others on our route, was full of grain and forage of all kinds. On approaching a walled town they were fired upon by Chinese Imperial troops, and after a short fight they returned, having captured two modern guns, a quantity of arms and ammunition, and eight flags. They also captured a regiment of infantry, but these they disarmed, bringing along the colonel as a prisoner.

OUR RECEPTION AT PAOTINGFU

[October 19th]

About two miles from Paotingfu the column was met by a procession of the mandarins, headed by the Provincial Treasurer, or [1]*Fantai*, of the district (since beheaded), who held a long palaver with the General, during which he stated that he had arranged a camping ground for the troops outside the city but hoped they would not be allowed inside the walls. It was agreed that he would be given three days in which to prepare quarters in the city for the troops and a meeting was held next day by the Allied Generals to decide on the fate of the place. A messenger was captured the next day bearing a letter from the Fantai in which he stated that the foreign devils were encamped outside the city, but that he (the Fantai) had not allowed them to come inside.

The morning after our arrival the Generals and their staffs made a formal entry into the famous Boxer city [20 October], where the inhabitants had never in their lives seen a foreigner before, except the few unfortunate missionaries, the last of whom—the Greens—were rescued a day or two before by the French. The day was bitterly cold, and it was pouring in torrents. As we rode through the narrow, filthy streets we wondered why we had come at all. There was nobody to fight. The Chinese soldiers were now supposed to be helping us in fighting the Boxers.

1. Also spelled *Fengtai*

The Punishment

It was difficult to believe that a few short months before refined English and American women had been dragged down these same streets without clothes, their homes burnt and their husbands shot before their eyes, and themselves exposed to all manner of insults before being finally massacred by the people who were now regarding us from the shelter of their shops. All of them a short time ago wore the Boxer uniform, but were now professedly our friends. It is satisfactory to state that the *Fantai*, or Chief Treasurer, who was known to have had a hand in the murder of several missionaries, was placed under arrest and afterwards beheaded, together with two others concerned. Several of the chief temples and four corners of the city walls were also blown up, and a heavy fine was levied on the city.

PUNISHING THE BOXERS:
WITH THE PAOTINGFU EXPEDITION [2]

[Tientsin–November 10, 1900]

During the expedition to Paotingfu, eighty miles to the south-west of Peking, the British advance guard halted at the walled town of Ting-Hsing [15 October]. The leading man of the town, who bore the reputation of being unfriendly towards foreigners, was kept under guard by a sentry of the Bengal Lancers until General Gaselee was able to receive him.

An everyday sight outside a walled town: the gruesome spectacle of heads of decapitated criminals hanging on the wall at the gate of a town is so common that we get accustomed to it. The victims are mostly thieves. A notification of the crime for which they have been punished is exhibited on the wall. The Chinese told us that the subject of my sketch were the heads of Boxers.

The French on the march to Paotingfu employed a number of camels for transport purposes, and these beasts proved their usefulness when the Peiho river was reached. The bridges hastily built by the Madras Sappers and Miners gave way after most of the troops had crossed, and the camels were of the greatest service in taking the baggage over the river, which had to be forded.

The village of Wang-tan was well known to be a Boxer centre. It was found to be entrenched and fortified. When the 3rd Bombay Cavalry reached the village, it was deserted, the Boxers having abandoned it some days previously. The place was fired by the Bombay Cavalry [23 October].

Receiving information that a fortified Boxer Village—Koosang—was within a few miles of Paotingfu, a detachment of infantry, a pom-pom battery, and a squadron of cavalry started out from Paoting on a three days punitive expedition [24 October]. The troops encountered no opposition and burnt the village, destroying some ammunition and arms. All the district round Paotingfu is an ideal country for cavalry, with its miles and miles of flat country with deep sunken roads.

EDITOR'S NOTE

Whiting departed from Paotingfu on 27 October and reached Tientsin on 6 November 1900. He travelled with his friends of the 3rd Bombay Cavalry. There was no fighting on this trip and so he was free to sketch the colorful scenes and interesting experiences which he observed en route. Once back in Tientsin, he filed his reports.

Whiting then returned to Peking, where he spent the winter of 1900-1901. He was fascinated by the "picturesqueness" of life in Peking, and on 10 March 1901 sent the following comment:

"Street merchants, donkey-boys, camel trains, rickshaws, and a continuous stream of Peking carts...jostle each other all day....The troops in their various uniforms, Western and Oriental, add greatly to the picturesqueness of the scene...."

He recorded ordinary life in Peking and the occasional events connected with the military occupation, such as the execution on 26 February 1901 of two prominent anti-foreign officials; the ceremony on 6 March to celebrate the impending departure of the New South Wales Contingent who were returning to Australia; and the ceremony on 10 March when the bodies of Allied soldiers who had died in action were moved from a temporary burial site within the British Legation compound to a larger cemetery outside the city walls.

By the end of March Whiting embarked at Taku for his return to England. He was in England by June, working once again as a staff artist covering local events for *The Daily Graphic*.

HERBERT HOOVER:
BESIEGED IN TIENTSIN

Herbert Clark Hoover, a man who in March 1929 became the 31st President of the United States, was a chance participant in the events which consumed North China, and the entire world, in the summer of 1900.

After graduating from Stanford University in 1895, Hoover had embarked on a career as a mining engineer. In 1898 he was working in Australia when a lucrative opportunity in China presented itself. He traveled from Australia to London in January 1899 to review details of the new position, in which he was to serve as Consulting Engineer to the Chinese Engineering and Mining Company, which was backed by London-based foreign capital.

He then proceeded to California, to marry his college sweetheart, Miss Lou Henry; the wedding took place at the home of her parents in Monterey, California on 10 February 1899. The couple set out for China on the following day, taking the *Coptic* for Yokohama and Shanghai; there they switched ships and took a small coastal steamship north to Taku, transferred to Tongku, then went by train to Peking.

After a brief series of meetings in Peking, the Hoovers returned to Tientsin and took up temporary residence in the Astor House, the leading hotel in Tientsin, on March 20, 1899. The newlyweds were each 25 years old, and in need of a house in Tientsin's Foreign Concession (also called the Settlement).

While Herbert Hoover went at once to tour various mines, Lou Hoover was left with the task of finding a house. She soon rented a spacious two-story house on Racecourse Road, located on the outskirts of the Settlement. This imposing western-style building required a staff of 15 Chinese servants! She also hired a Chinese language teacher and soon achieved reasonable fluency. She pursued her interest in photography, and whenever possible she traveled with her husband—even becoming the first Western female to actually descend into a Chinese mine.

Hoover home in Tientsin
Courtesy of the Herbert Hoover Presidential Library
West Branch, Iowa

In the fall of 1899 Hoover was given the added title of Mining Engineer-in-Chief to the Mining Bureau of Chihli and Jehol. This added responsibility required an expanded technical staff, and he hired five well-trained Western engineers as assistants. Together they covered a wide area of North China in their search for mining opportunities. However by the spring of 1900 the widespread threat from rural groups of Boxers forced Hoover to recall his experts to Peking.

Early in May 1900 Hoover was in the Western Hills near Peking, inspecting anthracite deposits, and his wife was visiting friends in Peking. Returning to the capital in the middle of May he discovered that Lou was ill, possibly seriously, and they returned at once to Tientsin to seek Western medical treatment. Doctors in Tientsin diagnosed her illness as a sinus infection, and by the end of May she was well enough to host a dinner at their home for Stanford graduates residing in China. Her sudden illness probably prevented the Hoovers from being besieged in Peking when railroad service from Peking to Tientsin ceased on 5 June.

As the political situation in North China worsened, the Hoovers could have moved south to Shanghai. Herbert Hoover decided to remain with his Chinese staff, and Lou Hoover refused to leave without her husband. On 17 June the Hoovers found themselves besieged in Tientsin.

Since the Hoover house was located beyond the mud wall which protected the south side of the Settlement, it was dangerously exposed when on Sunday 17 June the Chinese army on the outskirts of the city joined with the Boxers in bombarding the Foreign Concession. The Hoovers moved to the centrally-located residence of Edward B. Drew, an American who served as Commissioner of the Chinese Maritime Customs at Tientsin.

Hoover's engineering and organizational expertise was quickly exercised. He supervised the Chinese in erecting street barricades made from sacks of rice, sugar and peanuts taken from local warehouses; at night, under an armed escort, Hoover and his staff traveled outside the barricades to the city water plant in order to boil water for the besieged community. He also assumed responsibility for providing food to a large group of Chinese refugees who had sought refuge with the westerners.

Lou Hoover volunteered her services as a nurse at the hospital which had been established at the Tientsin Club. She traveled back and forth by bicycle, riding "close to the walls of buildings to avoid stray bullets" but even so, "one day she had a tire punctured by a bullet."

Siege conditions existed in Tientsin from 17 June until the Chinese Walled City was finally captured on 14 July 1900. Hoover played a small role in this capture by joining the Americans on the left flank of the advancing Allied army on 13 July. His knowledge of the countryside, obtained over the previous year while horseback riding with Lou, was useful to the Allied commanders.

With the siege ended, the Allied army began to make plans for the advance to Peking; and the Hoovers began to plan for their departure from China. Regular train service from Tientsin to Tongku was restored on 2 August, and the Hoovers departed for London on 4 August.

The Chinese Engineering and Mining Company, Hoover's employers, were controlled by Chinese, but its bonds were held by Europeans. The bondholders were naturally concerned when they discovered that many of the company assets had been seized by the Allied armies as they marched into North

China. Hoover successfully arranged for the assets to be signed over to a syndicate based in London. The Hoovers spent the fall of 1900 in London while details of the financial reorganization of the company were sorted out.

Hoover was sent back to China at the end of the year as General Manager of the new venture. The Hoovers reached Japan in January 1901 and Lou Hoover remained in Japan until April while Herbert hurried to China to take up his new assignment.

In the fall of 1901 a Belgian syndicate bought out the British. Hoover resigned, and by the end of the year the Hoovers were back in London. Herbert Hoover's career was about to take an enormous leap forward, and soon he would have offices in New York City and San Francisco as well as London. However his experience in the summer of 1900 in China provided an invaluable foundation for the task which catapulted him to worldwide recognition, securing food and clothing for the war-torn citizens of Belgium and France as Chairman of the Commission for Relief in Belgium from 1915 through 1917.

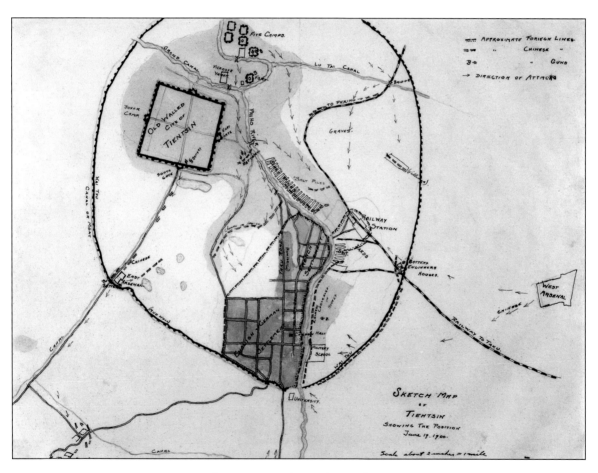

Map of Tientsin as drawn by Herbert Hoover
Courtesy of the Herbert Hoover Presidential Library West Branch, Iowa

Lou Hoover with Cannon
Courtesy of the Herbert Hoover Presidential Library West Branch, Iowa

LETTER POSTMARKED AUGUST 8, 1900
From Lou Hoover to Evelyn Wright

You missed one of the opportunities of your life by not coming to China in the summer of 1900. The very fact that the things have happened that have happened make it queer that your guardian star did not get you here in time for it. So many many many times I thought of you, and that you should have been here—at the most interesting siege and bombardment of the age. The men from Ladysmith—and we have them with us, *Terrible's* guns and all—say the bombardment there could not compare with ours. The loss of life was greater than either Kimberly or Mafeking. Only it was so short that we did not suffer from hunger—but neither did we have the chance of honorable, or otherwise, surrender before us in case hunger ever should come. We simply had to stand by our guns until the end; with one last bullet kept back for each one of ourselves. Our only hope was that the Chinese can't, won't, and don't charge—and they did not—to any alarming extent. So a good many hundred civilians and a couple of thousand troops sat still and repelled faint-hearted charges while 10,000 or 15,000 Chinese troops and 20,000 Boxers plunked shells of all sizes into us for exactly one week, without a sound or word from the outside reaching us.

Then the first relief cut their way into us, 2000 of them—enough to get in, but not to do anything more than we could when they got there. And for another two weeks we sat there while the relief came in from the south, at the rate of a thousand a day, more or less, while the Chinese gathered on the north more rapidly, and we gradually got to *exchanging* shells, instead of *receiving* them—and finally one day came when we *sent* but did not *receive*—and at the same time we, who can, will, and *do*, charge—*charged*. And now the only question is the relief of Peking. For more than a month we have had but two or three unreliable messages from there!

Do you realize it, that never have so many flags been in action together since our history began. Russian, Japanese, French, German, Austrian, Italian, English, and American! And such a motley array of troops—artillery cavalry, infantry, marines, sailors—Cossacks, Shiks, Siamese, a couple of English *Chinese* regiments on our side—a lot of our own darkies, who strike terror to the hearts of some.

But we are still living it—and just now they say *"kai fan"* which means tiffin is ready—and the ink is too bad to come back to it again—Goodbye for the nonce, dear one—I think I will see you soon—but oh, if you *had* been here!

ILLUSTRATION ART:
ENGLAND AND AMERICA

Illustrations 1 through 37 are from the
Jean S. and Frederic A. Sharf Collection
Chestnut Hill, Massachusetts

1. Taking Possession: A Guard of British Marines on the Island of Liu-Kung-Tao
Artist: Joseph Nash, Jr., from a photograph by Samuel P. Ferguson, RN
Published: 16 July 1898 in *The Graphic*
Size: 6 1/2" x 10"
Medium: Gouache with Chinese white highlights on board

The British marines are depicted casually, but in their official uniforms. No military action was required, as Japan had evacuated Weihaiwei earlier in May, after receiving the final payment from China of the indemnity owed from the Sino-Japan War peace settlement.

Liu-Kung-Tao was the largest of the islands at the entrance to the harbor of Weihaiwei. After the Japanese destroyed the mainland forts in February 1895 during the Sino-Japan War, they had established a military garrison and a naval dockyard on this island. Weihaiwei was an excellent strategic acquisition for Great Britain, giving her a naval base in North China to match the German base at Kiaochau and the Russian base at Port Arthur, each acquired in March 1898. It was also close to the mouth of the Peiho River, the access point for Tientsin and Peking.

Samuel P. Ferguson, Engineer on HMS *Narcissus*, arrived at Weihaiwei on 21 May 1898. This ship had been sent to hoist the British flag over the newly-acquired leasehold.

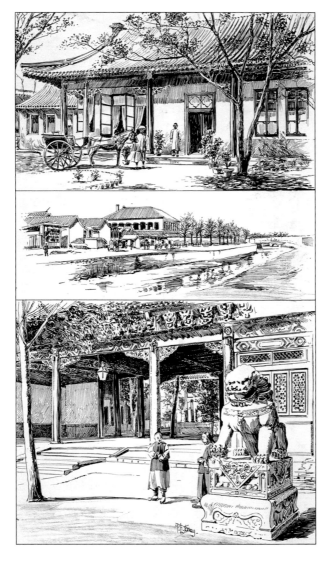

2. The British Quarters in Peking: Views at the Legation
Artist: P. F. Young, from photographs submitted by Reverend George Owen
Published: 27 June 1900 in *The Daily Graphic*
Size: 14" x 8"
Medium: Pen and ink on board

Three settings are depicted:
    a) The house of the Chinese Secretary, located within the British Legation Compound;
    b) The Legation Compound viewed from across an open space by the side of a canal;
    c) A guardian statue at the entrance to the house of the British Minister, located within the Compound.

The London Missionary Society.
East City Peking.

**3. The Peril in Peking: The London Missionary Society's Station in the East City,
Reported to have been Burned by the Boxers**

Artist: P. F. Young, from photographs submitted by Reverend George Owen
Published: 27 June 1900 in *The Daily Graphic*
Size: 9" x 11"
Medium: Pen and ink on board

Reverend George Owen had returned from Peking to London on leave in June 1900. When reports reached him that the London Missionary Society buildings in Peking had been burned by Boxers, he was able to supply the editors of *The Daily Graphic* with photos and descriptions of these buildings and of other significant places in Peking.

Various houses within the missionary compound are drawn and identified. The west entrance to the church within the compound is also depicted; this building was constructed in 1887 and was considered one of the finest Christian church buildings in North China. Looking at these buildings, it was obvious that the missionaries living in Peking within their various compounds were accustomed to a modern and comfortable lifestyle—in a city known for being dirty and lacking all sanitation.

4. Reinforcements for the Far East: Preparing Naval Drafts for China at Portsmouth
Artist: Joseph Nash, Jr., from a sketch by C. W. Cole, RN
Published: 7 July 1900 in *The Graphic*
Size: 6" x 10 1/2"
Medium: Pen and ink and gouache on board

Cole's drawing, probably submitted early in May 1900, was held by the editors until it could be reworked by one of their studio artists into a timely publishable drawing. By early July 1900 the interest in events in China was reaching a frenzy, and this illustration could then show the British public that the Navy was doing its best to send men properly outfitted to the China Station. Cole departed for China prior to the outbreak of actual conflict. By the middle of June he was already in the Far East; he served as Fleet Paymaster. He continued to submit drawings to *The Graphic*.

**5. The Crisis in China: With a Surveying Party from Canton to Hankow.
Illustration of a Street Scene in the Great Interior City of Chang Sha**

Artist: Herbert Johnson, from a photograph by an unidentified correspondent
Published: 7 August 1900 in *The Graphic*.
Size: 9" x 10"
Medium: Gouache on board

Chang Sha was a large commercial city located south of Wuhang in Hunan Province on the proposed railway line from Hankow to Canton. This line was meant to be a continuation of the Luhan Railway from Peking to Hankow. On 14 April 1898 the American China Development Company was given the concession to construct this railroad; surveying the route commenced in 1899.

The population of Chang Sha had a reputation for being totally independent and extremely anti-foreign. We can imagine the reception which western surveyors would have received! The construction of railways by the various western syndicates was viewed by the Chinese population as an intrusion into their traditional way of life and thus created fertile ground for the Boxers to sow their seeds of hatred of foreign influences.

6. General View of the Operations During the Attack on the Taku Forts on June 17

Artist: F. C. Dickinson, from a sketch by David Peacock, Chief Engineer, HMS *Alacrity*

Published: 11 August 1900 in *The Graphic*

Size: 6 1/2" x 11 1/2"

Medium: Gouache on board

Dickinson shows the climactic event on the morning of 17 June 1900. He had access to very accurate information about the events, as well as the locations of various allied ships and local landmarks such as the Imperial Dockyard in the left middle distance and the railway station at Tongku in the upper right. He was able to correctly depict the snake-like shape of the Peiho River.

The drawing was accompanied by the following text:

> When one of the batteries on the north side of the river had been stormed and carried by a British, Italian and Japanese landing party, the guns in it were immediately turned onto the forts on the south side of the river. At 6 a.m., a shell from this battery entered the magazine of the South Fort, causing a terrific explosion, the shock being strongly felt by the ships which were lying 13 miles off, outside the river. The explosion decided the fortunes of the day in favor of the Allies, and only desultory firing followed at lengthening intervals, until all the Forts were captured by 7 a.m.

HMS *Alacrity*, with Peacock on board, was part of the Allied Fleet lying 10 to 13 miles off shore in the Gulf of Pechihli.

7. The Siege of the British Legation at Peking: A Sortie
Artist: Joseph Nash, Jr. from a sketch by Captain Francis. G. Poole
Published: 13 October 1900 in *The Graphic*
Size: 11" x 14"
Medium: Gouache in dark grisaille on board

Poole's sketch depicted an event which took place on Friday 29 June 1900. On that day the besieged Westerners planned two sorties outside their fortified area, to deal with sources of Chinese gunfire. Each was to depart at 3 a.m. Poole was in command of one, and Captain Wray of the other. For some reason, Poole decided to submit a sketch of Wray's sortie, not his own.

Wray is shown leading his men through a breach in the wall of the British Legation Compound. Their objective was to cross the Mongol Market and seize a Chinese gun on the other side which had been directing heavy fire into the Compound. They reached their objective only to find that the Chinese had moved the gun. They then retreated, burning a few Chinese houses on their way back to the British Legation Compound.

While Wray is here depicted in a heroic way there was considerable questioning among the Legation inhabitants of his actual heroism. The British marines, Russian sailors, and volunteers who served under him in this sortie all agreed that he had hidden while urging them to charge!

8. Japanese Troops Advancing in the Cornfields at Pei-Tsang, August 5, 1900
Artist: unknown
Published: c. October/November 1900, unknown publication.
Size: 8 1/2" x 12 1/2"
Medium: Gouache on paper

The Allied Expeditionary Force left Tientsin on 4 August and fought their first engagement at Pei-Tsang early on the morning of 5 August. The Japanese troops, marching to the left of the city, became involved in severe fighting in the cornfields where Boxer soldiers were lying in ambush.

9. A Strange Spectacle in China's Forbidden City

Artist: Sydney Adamson
Published: 10 November 1900 in *Leslie's Weekly*
Size: 22" x 16"
Medium: Gouache on paper

Adamson had accompanied the Allied troops on the march to Peking. He was able to attend the Allied Victory Parade on 28 August, and was thus able to observe not only the parade itself but the tour which followed, gaining access to the Imperial Palace buildings within the Forbidden City. This drawing was accompanied by the following text:

Mandarins and Palace Attendants Serving Tea, Fruits, and Nuts to the Victorious Officers of the Allied Forces who had just Desecrated the Sacred City.

10. The Allied Forces in China: The Capture of Liang-Hsiang by Eight Hundred German Infantry and Forty-Five 1st Bengal Lancers

Artist: Amedee Forestier, from a sketch by the late Lionel Barff
Published: 1 December 1900 in *Illustrated London News*
Size: 10" x 14"
Medium: Gouache on board

Liang-hsiang-hsien was a walled town located 18 miles southwest of Peking, on the main road to Paotingfu. On 11 September 1900 the Allies attacked the town. As soon as the Allied heavy artillery began bombardment, the Boxers fled, taking the road south to Paotingfu.

This drawing depicts some of the fleeing Boxers being dispersed while the main body of Allied troops heads toward the town. About 30 armed Boxers were killed as they fled.

11. After the Relief of the Legations: Prince Ching Returns to Peking to Negotiate for Peace

Artist: George K. Jones, from a sketch by Fred Whiting
Published: 6 November 1900 in *The Daily Graphic*
Size: 12" x 11 1/2"
Medium: Pen and ink on board

On 3 September 1900 Prince Ching returned to Peking. Fred Whiting was a witness:

> He was met some three miles away from the North Gate of the city by a detachment of Japanese cavalry. While at the gate, where his soldiers were disbanded, a detachment of the 4th Bengal Lancers was waiting to take its place in the procession. The Prince's cavalcade has rather an appearance of dingy grandeur which, perhaps, may be accounted for by the evil times. The retinue were mounted on rough Mongol ponies and mules and consisted of one or two mandarins with soldiers and attendants, the rear being brought up by a train of Peking carts containing the women of the party. Prince Ching wore ordinary Chinese costume, not even wearing his red button cap and peacock feathers— the signs of high rank.

On 11 September 1900 the Allies were informed that Li Hung-Chang and Prince Ching had been invested with full powers to act as Plenipotentiaries in settling peace terms on behalf of the Emperor with the Allies.
Whiting's original sketch was also given to Frederic De Haenen to work up into a finished drawing— which was published as a double-page spread on Saturday, 10 November in *The Graphic*.

12. East and West: A Group of Officers at the Gate of the Forbidden City, Peking
Artist: Gordon Browne, from a sketch by a correspondent
Published: 8 December 1900 in *The Graphic*
Size: 13" x 17 1/2"
Medium: Gouache on board

This drawing was accompanied by the following text:

> Whatever the jealousies felt in Diplomatic quarters and fostered by the Press of rival Powers, the officers of the International troops are on the best of terms, fraternizing together most amicably.

Representative officers are depicted in groups, as follows: British and Japanese; Russian, German and American; French and Italian.

13. The "Handy" Man at Work in China: Repairing a Railway
Artist: Frank Dadd, from a sketch by a correspondent
Published: 15 December 1900 in *The Graphic*
Size: 11" x 14 1/2"
Medium: Gouache on board

The use of sailors for various tasks both in China and in South Africa earned them the nickname of "Handyman." This drawing shows men of the Naval Brigade starting the task of repairing the railroad. Since these men left China on 5 September, the drawing depicts their services over the months of July and August.

Once the siege ended on 14 August, General Gaselee had two priorities:

1) Reconnect the telegraph (completed on 17 August)
2) Reconstruct the railway from Peking to Tientsin in order to assure a smooth flow of men and supplies (not completed until early December).

14. With Sir Claude MacDonald on HMS *Endymion*: Divine Service on Sunday Morning
Artist: Frank Dadd, from a sketch by Robert Barr, RN
Published: 5 January 1901 in *The Graphic*
Size: 7 1/2" x 11"
Medium: Gouache on board

This drawing records a religious service on the quarterdeck of the ship on Sunday morning, 4 November 1900. Seated with Sir Claude and Lady MacDonald are Captain Callaghan, who commanded the ship, and Commander Boothby.

MacDonald had been replaced as British Minister at Peking by Sir Ernest Satow, who arrived in Peking on 20 October. The MacDonalds left Peking on 25 October and boarded HMS *Endymion* on 31 October. They sailed from Yokohama for a well-deserved vacation in England. Sir Claude subsequently returned to the Far East as British Minister at Tokyo.

Robert Barr, whose sketch formed the basis of this illustration, was an ordinary sailor on board the *Endymion*. He submitted numerous sketches to *The Graphic* during the three years he served on the China Station; this was sent from Nagasaki on 5 November, and was published two months later.

15. The International Commission of Enquiry into the Massacre at Paotingfu
Artist: Frank Dadd, from a sketch by a British Officer (possibly Captain Francis G. Poole)
Published: 19 January 1901 in *The Graphic Supplement*
Size: 13" x 11"
Medium: Gouache on board

This event took place in late October 1900 in the Viceroy's palace at Paotingfu. The *Fengtai*, or Provincial Treasurer, is shown pleading for his life by claiming that he was unable to cope with the Boxers and unable to prevent the massacre of missionaries at Paotingfu.

The three men seated at the table are, from left to right: Captain Poole, Great Britain; Major Von Brixen, Germany; Lieutenant Sambry, Italy. At the far left, an Australian soldier is guarding the Fengtai.

On 6 November the Fengtai was beheaded, along with the Governor of Paotingfu and the Commander of its military garrison.

The seated figure on the far right is not identified, nor is the standing officer in the middle.

**16. With the Allies in China: A Mixed Team of Cossacks and Coolies
Drawing an Ammunition Cart**
Artist: Frank Dadd, from a photograph by Max Rechnitzer
Published: 19 January 1901 in *The Graphic*
Size: 12" x 11"
Medium: Gouache on board

This drawing, worked up from a photograph submitted by a Russian officer, illustrates the Russian participation in the occupation of China after the relief of Peking. The Russians were assigned to guard the railway line which ran from Tongku to Shanhaikwan.

The drawing was used in *The Graphic* as a cover for the issue of Saturday, 19 January 1901, with no accompanying story. There were two important Russian punitive expeditions from Shanhaikwan—one on 16 October to Nikoo, the other on 5 November to Tongshan. It is not clear which was the source for the photo and the resulting drawing.

17. The Allies in China: An Act of Retribution
Artist: Percy F. S. Spence, from a sketch by Fred Whiting
Published: 16 February 1901 in *The Graphic*
Size: 8" x 14 1/2"
Medium: Gouache on board

Fred Whiting recorded this incident in his report as having taken place on 23 October, en route to Paotingfu. There was enormous interest in England in the Indian troops who were sent to China, since their previous usage had been primarily in India. The fact that they were able to perform with great success and great bravery was a source of pride which seemed to the British public a validation of empire. The novels and stories of Rudyard Kipling had created an environment within England for illustrations of Indian soldiers in action. It should be noted that while Indian troops had been sent to South Africa, they were not used in combat against the Boers; their use in actual combat in China was thus particularly novel and exciting.

The 3rd Bombay Cavalry was not part of the original troop allocation raised in India for service in China. They reached China in September 1900 to relieve the 1st Bengal Lancers, and were stationed at Matou. This drawing was accompanied by the following text:

The village of Wang-tan was well known to be a Boxer centre. It was found to be entrenched and fortified. When the 3rd Bombay Cavalry reached the village, it was deserted, the Boxers having abandoned it some days previously. The place was set on fire by the Bombay Cavalry.

18. The Return from Paotingfu: Tumbling in the Quicksand
Artist: Amedee Forestier, from a sketch by John Schonberg
Published: February 1901 in *Illustrated London News*
Size: 8 1/2" x 12 1/2"
Medium: Gouache on board

The Allied troops had gone to Paotingfu in October 1900 to punish that city for its support of the Boxers, and in particular to seek retribution for the massacre of Western missionaries which had taken place there in May 1900. With the successful conclusion of this expedition, General Alfred Gaselee determined that troops returning to Peking would travel in three separate columns, each taking a different route.

The column led by General Richardson stopped en route at Young-ch'ing-hsien on 31 October for two days in order to punish that city for its Boxer allegiances. On 3 November his column needed to cross the Hun-ho River, a broad, shallow stream with a bed of quicksand. Such a crossing was dangerous, as this drawing dramatically illustrates.

19. The Return from Paotingfu: With the Punitive Expedition on the March to Tientsin
Artist: Douglas Macpherson, from sketches by Fred Whiting
Published: 19 February 1901 in *The Daily Graphic*
Size: 12" x 11"
Medium: Pen and ink on board

With the successful conclusion of the Expedition to Paotingfu, one column of troops—commanded by Major General Lorne Campbell—returned to their base at Tientsin. In doing so they needed to cross the dangerous Yang-ho River. Fred Whiting accompanied the column and sent back several drawings with the following text:

> On the march back to Tientsin from Paotingfu, we had to cross the Yang-ho River. We commandeered Chinese to point out the ford. This they did, going up to their waists in water, and an experiment was made with two artillery wagons drawn by eight horses. After crossing, however, it was decided by General Lorne Campbell that the heavy guns could not be safely taken across owing to the treacherous nature of the river bed, so the wagons re-crossed and found another ford later in the day.

**20. The Allies in China: Looting in Peking. One of the Seventy
Wagon-loads of Plunder Sent to France and Subsequently Returned to China**
Artist: Frederic De Haenen, from a sketch by a correspondent (probably Fred Whiting)
Published: 2 March 1901 in *The Graphic*
Size: 7" x 10"
Medium: Gouache on board

French soldiers are accompanying a "Peking Cart" loaded with carefully packed wooden cases drawn by Chinese coolies. It was published with the following text:

> This great haul of spoil was taken from the Pagoda of Ancestors and sent to Marseilles
> by General Frey. It was sent back by order of the French Government.

Looting was prevalent among the soldiers of the Allied nations; there was a sense that it was justified as "spoils of war." Much of the loot remained in the West; little was actually returned. This drawing was published many months after Whiting had observed the event in Peking (probably September 1900). The news that the French were returning this loot certainly prompted its publication.

21. The Return from Paotingfu: Crossing the Yang-Ho River
Artist: Drawn by Fred Whiting on site
Published: 11 March 1901 in *The Daily Graphic*
Size: 7" x 9 1/2"
Medium: Pen and ink on paper

Whiting inscribed this drawing on the reverse as follows:

> In crossing the Yang-ho River, there were several exciting moments. The small Chinese ponies were falling into holes in the river bed. In my sketch, an Indian commissariat cart is stuck in the mud, and the pony rapidly sinking, but was eventually pulled out by the leading ponies and a group of Chinese coolies.

Correspondents like Whiting developed a technique for recording with pen and ink what they saw on the spot, then annotating their drawings with text on the reverse. This drawing was sent from China to London and was published exactly as Whiting had composed it (not redrawn by a studio artist).

22. The Allied Army in North China
Artist: Lieutenant Colonel Oswald Claude Radford, British Indian Army
Not Produced for Publication - Circa April 1901
Size: 24" x 18"
Medium: Watercolor on Paper

Radford, an amateur artist, has introduced into a busy street scene a careful depiction of Allied soldiers from various nations. From left to right they are: Japanese Infantryman of the 5th Hiroshima Division; French Zouave; Sikh of the 4th Punjab Infantry (Radford's own regiment); Italian Bersaglieri, with his cloak securely wrapped around him; member of the German East Asian Brigade with characteristic jaunty hat; Chinese soldier in a colorful regimental tunic; Russian Army officer in a handsome greatcoat; and a Cossack mounted on a pony.

Radford and his regiment arrived from India in September 1900 along with the 3rd Infantry Brigade under General Reid. They were assigned to quarters in Shanhaikwan, Chihli Province, where their primary responsibility was guarding the railroad line. He led his troops—along with men from other Allied nations—on successful punitive exhibitions in November 1900 and April 1901.

23. The Plague at Hong Kong: Frightening the Devil Away
Artist: Fred Whiting, from a sketch by a British Officer
Published: 27 July 1901 in *The Graphic*
Size: 8" x 12"
Medium: Gouache on board

Fred Whiting left China in March 1901 and returned to London. He was given numerous assignments—the first of which was to cover a horse show in Ireland. However he was repeatedly called upon over the next few years to use his knowledge of and travels in China to develop drawings sent to *The Graphic* from the Far East.

In this drawing, a news event (outbreak of plague in Hong Kong in June 1901) is the pretext for a dramatic drawing which seeks to convey some sense of Chinese religious beliefs and the colorful ceremonies which accompanied them. The accompanying text is as follows:

> During the past month the plague has been slowly but surely on the increase, and to such an extent that many are already prophesying the return of another serious epidemic of it. On two evenings recently, between sunset and 10 o'clock, the district of Wanchai...where the plague is most rife was converted into a most perfect pandemonium by the Chinese. Hundreds of them formed in procession and made the night hideous with the incessant and discordant din of their yells, crackers, reed instruments, gongs, bells, rattles drums and cymbals...to frighten the Devil away.

The British officer observed this scene in front of a Joss House, where a roast pig was also conspicuous as an offering to the Gods. He was amazed to find that even better classes of Chinese believed in "such inane superstitions."

24. Bank Holiday at Earl's Court: The Grand Military Spectacle
Artist: George Soper
Published: 10 August 1901 in *The Graphic*
Size: 11 1/2" x 15 1/2"
Medium: Gouache on board

This drawing was accompanied by the following text:

> The Military Exhibition at Earl's Court attracted large crowds on Bank Holiday. The story of the Relief of the Legations, as told in the Imperial Theatre, was greatly appreciated by packed audiences. Our illustration represents the Boxers gathering and exciting the mob before delivering an attack.

Bank Holiday weekend in England started on Saturday, 3 August 1901. The Military Exhibition at Earl's Court was a display of weapons combined with various theatrical offerings, accompanied by patriotic band music. It was open from 11 a.m. until 11 p.m. each day; the China spectacle was the feature event with two daily shows, at 3:30 and 8:30 p.m. It was so popular that it remained open for some time after the initial weekend.

It is significant to note that in August 1901 there was still enormous interest in Britain about China in general and the Boxers in particular.

25. Punishment for Piracy at Chefoo
Artist: George Soper, from a photograph.
Published: 17 August 1901 in *The Graphic*
Size: 6" x 8 1/2"
Medium: Gouache on board

Chefoo—located on the Gulf of Pechihli in the province of Shantung—was an important center for trade, which circulated north to Tientsin and south to Shanghai, as well as east across the Gulf to Port Arthur and Korea. Merchandise was carried by coastal vessels, cargo junks operated by Chinese merchants.

In the spring of 1901 the residue of Boxer aggression continued to manifest itself in an outbreak of piracy in the Gulf of Pechihli, which was so severe that trade at Chefoo was threatened. The Governor of Shantung ordered the Taotai at Chefoo to organize an expedition against the pirates operating along the coast, and they returned with 32 captured pirates.

According to *The Graphic*, "Thousands of Chinese crowded the Customs Jetty to witness the transportation of the pirates to the Taotai's Yamen." Beheading was the requisite punishment for piracy, and the spectacle was a popular recreation for Chinese and also for Westerners.

A public execution was held on 28 May at the Old Customs Jetty, and 11 confessed pirates were beheaded. Since there was no public executioner at Chefoo, ordinary cattle butchers were hired and provided with enough wine to intoxicate them into performing this task. With inferior swords, and intoxicated with wine, they required as many as five or six blows per man to accomplish the task. The corpses, with heads detached, were left on public view until noon.

The colorful and barbarous aspects of the spectacle are clearly shown in this drawing.

26. Farewell Dinner and Tatoo in Weihaiwei to Admiral Seymour
Artist: George Soper, from a sketch by Reverend F. McClymont
Published: 24 August 1901 in *The Graphic*
Size: 6 1/2" x 12"
Medium: Gouache on board

On 21 June 1901 a farewell dinner was held in Weihaiwei to honor Admiral Seymour, who was to return to England after Vice Admiral Sir Cyprian Bridge took over command of the China Station on 26 June. It was held at the cricket pavilion, an old Chinese building which had been specially decorated with flags and bunting for the occasion.

The log of HMS *Goliath* recorded that the dinner and ball were hosted by officers of the fleet who had served under Seymour. "A guard of honour was formed by bluejackets from the fleet and searchlights were displayed until after midnight." While dinner proceeded, a group of 80 marines and sailors organized a tatoo, illuminated by Chinese lanterns and attended by a large crowd.

Vice Admiral Bridge did not arrive until 25 June, and the official transfer was made on 26 June. Seymour departed for Hong Kong in his flagship, HMS *Centurion*, on 26 June and arrived at Portsmouth, England in August 1901.

27. Japanese Fleet Review, Kurahama Harbor, Near Uraga, July 14, 1901: In Honor of the Unveiling of the Monument to Commodore Perry at Uraga by the Japanese Government
Artist: Henry Reuterdahl.
Publication: date and place not known.
Size: 12" x 20"
Medium: Watercolor on paper

Ships from many nations assembled off the coast of Japan on 14 July 1901 under rainy and cloudy conditions, with choppy waters, for the ceremony which took place at noon. Reuterdahl has depicted the Japanese battleship HIJM *Hatsuse* with a companion torpedo boat of the Normand type. In the background on the left side is the Japanese battleship HIJM *Shikishima*. A contemporary eyewitness called these "two of the most modern battleships afloat."

As a result of her victory over China in the Sino-Japan War, and the resulting substantial financial indemnity, Japan was in an excellent position to embark on a total modernization of her fleet. Japan ordered and accepted delivery on four battleships, six armoured cruisers, and thirty torpedo boats between 1896 and 1900. Most of these were built in England.

The performance of Japanese soldiers on the Allied Expeditionary Force in the summer of 1900 was so outstanding that world attention began to focus on the concomitant development of her navy. Within a few years this navy would astound the world by its total victory over the Russians at Tsushima in May 1905—the culminating event of the Russo-Japan War.

28. Oriental 'Arries: A Street Scene in Peking
Artist: Fred Whiting
Published: 26 October 1901 in *The Graphic*
Size: 11" x 14"
Medium: Gouache on board

Whiting remained in Peking for almost seven months, from September 1900 through March 1901. He was fascinated by all aspects of the colorful, exotic life around him, even as he concentrated on his primary purpose for being there, which was to depict the Allied occupation. Whiting wrote the following text to accompany this drawing:

> Despite its ancient civilisation and the boasted culture of its inhabitants, the Celestial City rejoices in a large class resembling our Arries, one of whose chief delights is to gather in small companies on ponies or donkeys and gallop up and down the main street, covering the pedestrians with a cloud of thick black dust. During the recent occupation they were much in evidence, wearing silks and furs with their old padded clothes, and smoking cigarettes.

"Arries" were loud, noisy, even wild, but generally not dangerous.

**29. A Sharp Contest on the China Station: Curio Selling on Board a
Man-of-War at Kiu-Kiang**

Artist: Fred Whiting, from a sketch by B. G. Tomkins, RN
Published: 26 October 1901 in *The Graphic*
Size: 7" x 12 1/2"
Medium: Gouache on board

Kiu-kiang was one of four Treaty Ports on the Yangtse River. After the suppression of the Boxers the British decided to leave one powerful warship at each of these ports: Chin-kiang, Nanking, Kiu-kiang, and Hankow.

In addition, during the summer of 1901 HMS *Endymion* made a cruise up the Yangtse in order to impress the Chinese with British naval strength. This ship, a First Class Twin Screw Cruiser, was larger by 2000 tons than any warship previously seen at these ports, and thus drew large crowds at each port. B. G. Tompkins was an ordinary sailor on the *Endymion*; he submitted other sketches which *The Graphic* published. The following text accompanied the drawing:

> As a rule, before leaving a foreign station, our bluejackets made it a practice to get together all sorts and kinds of curios. On the China Station a general run is made on old china and silk. The native traders come on board and usually ask about ten times the value of the article, with the result that there is a job to beat them down. The best way to get over them is to walk away when you are half way through the bargain. They will very soon come down.

This drawing was published on the same page as Whiting's drawing of "Oriental 'Arries." Four weeks later *The Graphic* published another of Tomkins's submissions, this time a sketch of British sailors and marines on ponies at Nanking heading for the Ming Tombs.

30. The Boxers in a New Role: The Outbreak of Brigandage in China
Artist: Fred Whiting, from a sketch by a British Officer
Published: 26 October 1901 in *The Daily Graphic*
Size: 7 1/2" x 10"
Medium: Pen and ink on paper

This drawing depicts soldiers of the army of Yuan Shih Kai, bringing back a group of bound prisoners to Manton Tsun. The accompanying caption explained that "the country around the Summer Palace has been lately infested with brigands, former Boxers, broken bannermen, and burnt-out villagers."

Yuan Shih Kai was Governor of Shantung Province from 1899 until November 1901, when he was named to succeed Li Hung Chang (who had died in that month) in the more powerful position of Viceroy of Chihli. Yuan had proven himself an able administrator in Shantung, collecting taxes so efficiently that he was able to organize his own army of 20,000 soldiers. He used this powerful army to patrol the countryside and arrest troublemakers of all kinds. His troops were considerably more effective at this task than those of the Chinese Imperial Army.

31. A Chinese Game: Boys Playing Yah Ting at Hong Kong

Artist: Fred Whiting, from a sketch by Frederick W. I. Airey, RN
Published: 16 November 1901 in *The Daily Graphic*
Size: 9" x 12"
Medium: Gouache on board

This drawing was published with the following text:

> During the cold months at Hong Kong and Canton, when the Chinese 'boy' is not spending his spare time and his spare cash in gambling, he is playing the game of 'Yah Ting.' This game is played with an ordinary shuttlecock and the feet are used instead of a battledore. A group of 'boys' form a circle, and with marvelous dexterity—especially in their back kicks—keep the shuttlecock spinning up in the air.

Frederick W. I. Airey, a skillful artist who submitted many drawings to *The Graphic* during his service on the China Station, was Paymaster on HMS *Goliath*, which was stationed at Hong Kong from 14 February through 15 April 1901. This drawing probably depicts a scene he observed in February 1901.

32. Back to their Battered Capital: Homecoming Mandarins Passing the Chien Men Main Arch, Peking

Artist: Fred Whiting, from a sketch by a British Officer
Published: 23 November 1901 in *The Daily Graphic*
Size: 6" x 10"
Medium: Pen and ink on board

On 7 September 1901 a final peace protocol was signed by the Allied powers and the Imperial government. Foreign troops began to evacuate Peking, except for legation guards which each nation was permitted at their respective legation compounds. The Forbidden City and the Summer Palace were officially returned to the Chinese. In such a context, the Chinese mandarins returned to Peking.

33. A Visit to Korea: A Street Scene in Seoul
Artist: Frank Dadd, from a sketch by a British Officer
Published: 23 November 1901 in *The Graphic*
Size: 7" x 11"
Medium: Gouache on board

The Allied nations who had successfully defeated the Boxers were all concerned about the security of their nationals in China and the stability of conditions for expanded trade. Therefore, they increased the strength of their naval presence on what was known as the China Station. Warships now routinely visited the Korean port of Chemulpo as part of their tour of duty; and it was a short journey from the seaport to the capital city of Seoul.

Koreans were relatively recent additions to the general assortment of racial types to be observed in the Far East, and thus there was a fascination which this drawing captures. The following text accompanied the drawing:

> The Koreans are stalwart, well built, and bear themselves with a manly air, though lazy and of rather a timid expression. The hair is worn long, but is twisted into a top-knot, which is protected by the crown of a tall hat made of horsehair.

This drawing was published with a companion drawing of Korean aristocrats (known as *Yangbans*) competing at archery, their favorite sport. This drawing is significant for the prominent placement of two Japanese soldiers, symbolic of the special role which Japan played in the internal life of Korea.

**34. The Withdrawal of the Allies from Peking: Handing Over the
Forbidden City to the Chinese**

Artist: Fred Whiting, from a sketch by a British Officer
Published: 30 November 1901 in *The Graphic*
Size: 6" x 11"
Medium: Pen and ink with grey wash and Chinese white, on board

The Peace Protocol was signed on 7 September 1901, and the Allies now returned to the Chinese their Imperial and sacred buildings. The following text accompanied this drawing:

> In consequence of the signing of the Peace Protocol, Imperial buildings in and near Peking have been handed over to the Chinese by the Allies. Our illustration shows some Chinese officials taking over the Forbidden City. The troops on the right of the picture are some of those trained by Europeans, at the request of Yuan Shih Kai, Li Hung Chang's successor. In the centre of the picture facing the Chinese are a detachment of Japanese, while on the extreme left are some American troops.

35. "Keep the Door Open John"
Artist: Alexander Stuart Boyd
Published: 15 February 1902 in *The Daily Graphic*
Size: 11 1/2" x 14"
Medium: Pen and ink on board

The Anglo-Japan Alliance was signed on 31 January 1902, and this cartoon expressed the British concern that China remain open for commercial trade. The following caption accompanied this drawing:

The objects of the Alliance are in the first place to maintain the status quo in the Far East, and in the second place they are the maintenance of that commercial policy which is for convenience usually described as the policy of the Open Door...a third object is the maintenance of peace in that part of the world.

36. A Weird Buddhist Ceremony: A Devil Dance in Peking
Artist: Fortunino Matania, from a sketch by Captain Francis G. Poole
Published: 8 November 1902 in *The Graphic*
Size: 14" x 11"
Medium: Gouache on board

Captain Poole visited the Lamasary of Eternal Peace in the northwest section of the Tartar City of Peking, which became a popular tourist attraction after the Relief of Peking. Prior to the Boxer Rebellion this temple was extremely difficult for a westerner to enter. The lamasary was inhabited by approximately 1500 Mongolian and Tibetan lamas under the leadership of the Living Buddha.

Here Poole observed the dance of young monks disguised as devils. The dance was meant to attract a large crowd of Chinese who would witness the triumph of Good over Evil.

In this drawing a procession is seen headed by four monks disguised as white devils with masks, while others wore stag and sheep heads. The procession is followed by lamas with cymbals, drums, and long trumpets borne by two men. The devils are dancing to the accompaniment of discordant music; they dance faster and faster until the Living Buddha appears on a chair carried by eight monks and then the devils flee. The lamas then rejoice with loud music, dancing, and burning of incense.

37. The Anglo-Japanese Alliance: British Naval Officers at a Japanese Review at Hiroshima

Artist: Frank Dadd, from a sketch by Francis G. Cavanagh, RN (Clerk, HMS Glory)
Published: 17 January 1903 in *The Graphic*
Size: 11" x 14 1/2"
Medium: Gouache on board

HMS *Glory* was the flagship of the British China Station fleet. It was commanded by Vice Admiral Sir Cyprian Bridge. On 11 October 1902 the Glory docked at the Kure Naval Base, located on the Inland Sea of Japan, and remained there for one week.

Hiroshima was the headquarters of the 5th Army Division, the Japanese unit which took part in military operations in North China during the summer of 1900. These troops had marched side by side with men of the British army and navy, providing a strong basis for the camaraderie expressed in this drawing.

On this occasion the British officers were invited to attend an army troop review at Hiroshima. On the morning scheduled for the review, the officers of HMS *Glory* departed by boat for Ujina, the seaport of Hiroshima, and then travelled in a procession of jinrikshas to inspect the Military College at Hiroshima. After lunch at the Military Club they proceeded another two miles to the parade ground where the review of Japanese infantry, cavalry, and artillery took place.

This unprecedented exchange of hospitality was made possible by the Anglo-Japan Treaty which had been signed on 31 January 1902.

ILLUSTRATION ART: JAPAN

Illustrations 1 through 12 are from the
Jean S. and Frederic A. Sharf Collection
Museum of Fine Arts, Boston, MA

1. True Record of Chinese Telegraph: Secretary Sugiyama Fighting Desperately
Artist: Adachi Ginko
Published: June 1900
Size: 14" x 28"
Medium: Woodblock print

On the afternoon of 11 June 1900, the Chancellor of the Japanese Legation at Peking volunteered to go to the railroad station at Machiapu in order to determine if Seymour's relief column had arrived. Dressed in proper diplomatic attire, and unarmed except for an umbrella, Sugiyama traveled to the station which was located outside the city walls. He reached the station safely, but found no trains had arrived.

On his return in the early evening he was attacked at the South Gate by troops of General Tung. He was stripped naked and hacked to death.

2. The Allied Army Occupying a Fort at Taku
Artist: Adachi Ginko
Published: June 1900
Publisher: Fukuda Kumajiro
Size: 14" x 28"
Medium: Woodblock print

Captain Hattori is depicted leading the Japanese troops up toward the ramparts of the Northwest Fort at Taku. The Western troops are following.

3. The Japanese Army Occupying a Fort at Taku
Artist: Adachi Ginko
Published: June 1900
Size: 14" x 28"
Medium: Woodblock Print

Captain Hattori of the Japanese Navy is depicted leading his troops over the ramparts of the Northwest Fort in the early morning hours of 17 June 1900.

4. Events of the Boxers in China
Artist: Unknown
Published: 25 June 1900
Publisher: Kasai Torajiro, Seiundo Company, Kanda, Tokyo
Size: 15" x 28"
Medium: Color lithograph on paper

This print was meant to provide Japanese citizens with a summary of events which had taken place in China from 11 June 1900 (death of Secretary Sugiyama) to the capture of the Taku Forts.

Top row: Missionaries massacred by Chinese; Hattori's Brave Fight at the Taku Forts on 17 June.
Middle row: Railroad repairs by Allied Navy as Seymour advances; Conference of the Allied
              Commanders on 16 June; Murder of Sugiyama on 11 June.
Bottom row: Bombardment of Taku Forts on 17 June.

5. The Allied Army and Navy Forces Attacking the Taku Forts
Artist: Unknown
Published: 24 June 1900
Publisher: Ariyama Tomekichi, Kanda, Tokyo
Size: 15" x 28"
Medium: Color lithograph on paper

This print depicts the exchange of heavy gunfire in the early morning of 17 June, 1900. The Chinese opened fire at 12:50 a.m. from the Taku Forts on the Allied fleet anchored in the Gulf of Pechihli. Allied ships responded within a few minutes.

6. The Allied Armies Occupying the Taku Forts: The Brave Fight of Lieutenant Shiraishi

Artist: Unknown
Published: 27 June 1900
Publisher: Kasai Torajiro, Seiundo Company, Kanda, Tokyo
Size: 15" x 28"
Medium: Color lithograph on paper

Lieutenant Shiraishi took command of the Japanese troops after the death of Captain Hattori. He completed the conquest of the Northwest Forts at Taku.

7. The Japanese Soldiers Capturing a Fort at Taku
Artist: Unknown
Published: 28 June 1900
Publisher: Tanaka Kichigoro, Shoseido Company, Nihonbashi, Tokyo
Size: 15" x 28"
Medium: Color lithograph on paper

The Japanese troops under Captain Hattori of the Japanese Navy are depicted as they raced towards the Northwest Fort at Taku in the early morning of 17 June 1900. The guns of the fort were silenced by 4:30 a.m., which encouraged the Japanese and British to attack. Hattori was determined that his men would be the first to enter the fort. He was ably assisted by Lieutenant Shiraishi, who is also depicted.

8. The Occupation of the Taku Forts: Captain Hattori's Brave Fight
Artist: Unknown
Published: 1 July 1900
Publisher: Watanabe Tadahisa, Nihonbashi, Tokyo
Size: 15" x 28"
Medium: Color lithograph on paper

Captain Hattori pushed his Japanese troops to be first into the Taku Forts. As he reached the rampart of the Northwest Fort, leading his men, he was killed as he turned to assist the British commander over the ramparts. Hattori is shown here by himself, bravely urging his men over the walls.

9. The Battle at Tientsin Arsenal
Artist: Unknown
Published: 1 July 1900
Publisher: Kasai Torajiro, Seiundo Company, Kanda, Tokyo
Size: 15" x 28"
Medium: Color lithograph on paper

The Allied Relief Column entered Tientsin on 23 June 1900. Telegraphic communication was now restored, enabling news to reach Tokyo quickly. Printmakers could thus react in a timely manner to news from the battlefields. This print depicts the Western Arsenal at Tientsin in flames. The Arsenal was captured on 25 June, 1900.

10. The Siege and the Attack on the Tientsin Castle

Artist: Unknown
Published: 30 July 1900
Publisher: Kasai Torajiro, Seiundo Company, Kanda, Tokyo
Size: 15" x 28"
Medium: Color lithograph on paper

At 3:30 a.m. on 13 July 1900, the Allied armies left the Foreign Settlement at Tientsin in order to lay siege to the Chinese City (called Tientsin Castle by the Japanese, since it was a walled city). The American, British, French and Japanese troops were responsible for opening the South Gate.

This print depicts the Japanese commander, General Fukushima, conferring with the British commander, General Dorward, and the French commander, Colonel Pelacot. In the middle distance are troops of the Japanese 11th Infantry, American 9th Infantry, and British and French troops, all advancing towards the walled city in the distance.

11. Second Lieutenant Ota, 5th Cavalry Regiment, Charging a Village near Tientsin Castle
Artist: Unknown
Published: 8 August 1900
Publisher: Kasai Torajiro, Seiundo Company, Kanda, Tokyo
Size: 15" x 28"
Medium: Color lithograph on paper

On the afternoon of 13 July, General Fukushima became concerned that the Chinese might try to attack the Allies from the rear. He sent a detachment of cavalry under Lieutenant Ota to reconnoitre. They ran into some resistance at a village on the outskirts of the Chinese City, as shown in this print.

12. General Attack on the Tientsin Castle by the Allied Armies: The Hakko-tai Corps of the 11th Regiment Opening the South Inner Gate and Charging

Artist: Unknown
Published: 8 August 1900
Publisher: Kasai Torajiro, Seiundo Company, Kanda, Tokyo
Size: 15" x 28"
Medium: Color lithograph on paper

The action on 13 July was not conclusive. Japanese engineers were assigned the task of blowing up the South Gate in the early morning of 14 July. By 4 a.m. the Allied troops were able to enter the Chinese City and take possession of it. This print depicts the successful charge of Japanese soldiers through the South Gate.

ILLUSTRATION ART: ENGLAND AND AMERICA
(Chronological by publication date)
From Jean S. and Frederic A. Sharf Collection
Chestnut Hill, Massachusetts

1. **"Taking Possession: A Guard of British Marines on the Island of Liu-Kung-Tao"**

   Artist: Joseph Nash, Jr., from a photograph by Samuel P. Ferguson, RN
   Published: 16 July 1898 in *The Graphic*

2. **"The British Quarters in Peking: Views at the Legation"**

   Artist: P. F. Young, from photographs submitted by Reverend George Owen
   Published: 27 June 1900 in *The Daily Graphic*

3. **"The Peril in Peking: The London Missionary Society's Station in the East City, Reported to have been Burned by the Boxers"**

   Artist: P. F. Young, from photographs submitted by Reverend George Owen
   Published: 27 June 1900 in *The Daily Graphic*

4. **"Reinforcements for the Far East: Preparing Naval Drafts for China at Portsmouth"**

   Artist: Joseph Nash, Jr., from a sketch by C. W. Cole, RN
   Published: 7 July 1900 in *The Graphic*

5. **"The Crisis in China: With a Surveying Party from Canton to Hankow. Illustration of a Street Scene in the Great Interior City of Chang Sha"**

   Artist: Herbert Johnson, from a photograph by an unidentified correspondent
   Published: 7 August 1900 in *The Graphic.*

6. **"General View of the Operations During the Attack on the Taku Forts on June 17"**

   Artist: F. C. Dickinson, from a sketch by David Peacock, Chief Engineer, HMS Alacrity
   Published: 11 August 1900 in *The Graphic*

7. **"The Siege of the British Legation at Peking: A Sortie"**

   Artist: Joseph Nash, Jr. from a sketch by Captain Francis. G. Poole
   Published: 13 October 1900 in *The Graphic*

8. **"Japanese Troops Advancing in the Cornfields at Pei-Tsang, August 5, 1900"**

   Artist: unknown
   Published: c. October/November 1900, unknown publication.

9. **"A Strange Spectacle in China's Forbidden City"**

   Artist: Sydney Adamson
   Published: 10 November 1900 in Leslie's Weekly

10. **"The Allied Forces in China: The Capture of Liang-Hsiang by Eight Hundred German Infantry and Forty-Five 1st Bengal Lancers"**

    Artist: Amedee Forestier, from a sketch by the late Lionel Barff
    Published: 1 December 1900 in *Illustrated London News*

11. **"After the Relief of the Legations: Prince Ching Returns to Peking to Negotiate for Peace"**

    Artist: George K. Jones, from a sketch by Fred Whiting
    Published: 6 November 1900 in *The Daily Graphic*

12. **"East and West: A Group of Officers at the Gate of the Forbidden City, Peking"**

    Artist: Gordon Browne, from a sketch by a correspondent
    Published: 8 December 1900 in *The Graphic*

13. **"The 'Handy' Man at Work in China: Repairing a Railway"**
    Artist: Frank Dadd, from a sketch by a correspondent
    Published: 15 December 1900 in *The Graphic*

14. **"With Sir Claude MacDonald on HMS *Endymion*: Divine Service on Sunday Morning"**
    Artist: Frank Dadd, from a sketch by Robert Barr, RN
    Published: 5 January 1901 in *The Graphic*

15. **"The International Commission of Enquiry into the Massacre at Paotingfu"**
    Artist: Frank Dadd, from a sketch by a British Officer (possibly Captain Francis G. Poole)
    Published: 19 January 1901 in *The Graphic Supplement*

16. **"With the Allies in China: A Mixed Team of Cossacks and Coolies Drawing an Ammunition Cart"**
    Artist: Frank Dadd, from a photograph by Max Rechnitzer
    Published: 19 January 1901 in *The Graphic*

17. **"The Allies in China: An Act of Retribution"**
    Artist: Percy F. S. Spence, from a sketch by Fred Whiting
    Published: 16 February 1901 in *The Graphic*

18. **"The Return from Paotingfu: Tumbling in the Quicksand"**
    Artist: Amedee Forestier, from a sketch by John Schonberg
    Published: February 1901 in *Illustrated London News*

19. **"The Return from Paotingfu: With the Punitive Expedition on the March to Tientsin"**
    Artist: Douglas Macpherson, from sketches by Fred Whiting
    Published: 19 February 1901 in *The Daily Graphic*

20. **"The Allies in China: Looting in Peking. One of the Seventy Wagon-loads of Plunder Sent to France and Subsequently Returned to China"**
    Artist: Frederic De Haenen, from a sketch by a correspondent (probably Fred Whiting)
    Published: 2 March 1901 in *The Graphic*

21. **"The Return from Paotingfu: Crossing the Yang-Ho River"**
    Artist: Drawn by Fred Whiting on site
    Published: 11 March 1901 in *The Daily Graphic*

22. **"The Allied Army in North China"**
    Artist: Lieutenant Colonel Oswald Claude Radford, British Indian Army
    Not produced for publication - Circa April 1901

23. **"The Plague at Hong Kong: Frightening the Devil Away"**
    Artist: Fred Whiting, from a sketch by a British Officer
    Published: 27 July 1901 in *The Graphic*

24. **"Bank Holiday at Earl's Court: The Grand Military Spectacle"**
    Artist: George Soper
    Published: 10 August 1901 in *The Graphic*

25. **"Punishment for Piracy at Chefoo"**
    Artist: George Soper, from a photograph.
    Published: 17 August 1901 in *The Graphic*

26. "Farewell Dinner and Tatoo in Weihaiwei to Admiral Seymour"

Artist: George Soper, from a sketch by Reverend F. McClymont
Published: 24 August 1901 in *The Graphic*

27. "Japanese Fleet Review, Kurahama Harbor, Near Uraga, July 14, 1901: In Honor of the Unveiling of the Monument to Commodore Perry at Uraga by the Japanese Government"

Artist: Henry Reuterdahl.
Publication: date and place not known.

28. "Oriental 'Arries: A Street Scene in Peking"

Artist: Fred Whiting
Published: 26 October 1901 in *The Graphic*

29. "A Sharp Contest on the China Station: Curio Selling on Board a Man-of-War at Kiu-Kiang"

Artist: Fred Whiting, from a sketch by B. G. Tomkins, RN
Published: 26 October 1901 in *The Graphic*

30. "The Boxers in a New Role: The Outbreak of Brigandage in China"

Artist: Fred Whiting, from a sketch by a British Officer
Published: 26 October 1901 in *The Daily Graphic*

31. "A Chinese Game: Boys Playing *Yah Ting* at Hong Kong"

Artist: Fred Whiting, from a sketch by Frederick W. I. Airey, RN
Published: 16 November 1901 in *The Daily Graphic*

32. "Back to their Battered Capital: Homecoming Mandarins Passing the Chien Men Main Arch, Peking"

Artist: Fred Whiting, from a sketch by a British Officer
Published: 23 November 1901 in *The Daily Graphic*

33. "A Visit to Korea: A Street Scene in Seoul"

Artist: Frank Dadd, from a sketch by a British Officer
Published: 23 November 1901 in *The Graphic*

34. "The Withdrawal of the Allies from Peking: Handing Over the Forbidden City to the Chinese"

Artist: Fred Whiting, from a sketch by a British Officer
Published: 30 November 1901 in *The Graphic*

35. "Keep the Door Open John"

Artist: Alexander Stuart Boyd
Published: 15 February 1902 in *The Daily Graphic*

36. "A Weird Buddhist Ceremony: A Devil Dance in Peking"

Artist: Fortunino Matania, from a sketch by Captain Francis G. Poole
Published: 8 November 1902 in *The Graphic*

37. "The Anglo-Japanese Alliance: British Naval Officers at a Japanese Review at Hiroshima"

Artist: Frank Dadd, from a sketch by Francis G. Cavanagh, RN (Clerk, HMS *Glory*)
Published: 17 January 1903 in *The Graphic*

ILLUSTRATION ART: JAPAN
From the Jean S. and Frederic A. Sharf Collection
Museum of Fine Arts, Boston, Massachusetts

1. "True Record of Chinese Telegraph: Secretary Sugiyama Fighting Desperately"
   Artist: Adachi Ginko
   Published: June 1900

2. "The Allied Army Occupying a Fort at Taku"
   Artist: Adachi Ginko
   Published: June 1900

3. "The Japanese Army Occupying a Fort at Taku"
   Artist: Adachi Ginko
   Published: June 1900

4. "Events of the Boxers in China"
   Artist: Unknown
   Published: 25 June 1900

5. "The Allied Army and Navy Forces Attacking the Taku Forts"
   Artist: Unknown
   Published: 24 June 1900

6. "The Allied Armies Occupying the Taku Forts: The Brave Fight of Lieutenant Shiraishi"
   Artist: Unknown
   Published: 27 June 1900

7. "The Japanese Soldiers Capturing a Fort at Taku "
   Artist: Unknown
   Published: 28 June 1900

8. "The Occupation of the Taku Forts: Captain Hattori's Brave Fight"
   Artist: Unknown
   Published: 1 July 1900

9. "The Battle at Tientsin Arsenal"
   Artist: Unknown
   Published: 1 July 1900

10. "The Siege and the Attack on the Tientsin Castle"
    Artist: Unknown
    Published: 30 July 1900

11. "Second Lieutenant Ota, 5th Cavalry Regiment, Charging a Village near Tientsin Castle"
    Artist: Unknown
    Published: 8 August 1900

12. "General Attack on the Tientsin Castle by the Allied Armies: The Hakko-tai Corps of the 11th Regiment Opening the South Inner Gate and Charging"
    Artist: Unknown
    Published: 8 August 1900

BIOGRAPHICAL SKETCHES OF THE ARTISTS

Adamson, Sydney
Born in Dundee, Scotland. Trained in London. Exhibited at the Royal Academy, London. Worked during 1890s as an illustrator for various British magazines. In 1899 he was in the Philippines working for *Leslie's Weekly*, and also sending back articles to other American magazines.

Boyd, Alexander Stuart (1854-1930)
Born in Glasgow, Scotland. Painter of landscapes and genre subjects; illustrator of books, magazines and newspapers. Known for humorous drawings and political cartoons.

Browne, Gordon Frederick (1858-1932)
Born in Barnstead, Surrey. Studied at the Heatherley School, London. Began exhibiting landscapes at various London galleries, and the Royal Academy, in 1886. Illustrator of books and magazines. Produced a number of Boer War drawings.

Dadd, Frank (1858-1932)
Born in London. Came from a family of artists. Studied at South Kensington School and the Royal Academy. Began exhibiting at the Royal Academy in 1878. Known for black and white illustration of children's adventure novels, as well as for illustration of various colonial wars, especially the Boer War.

De Haenen, Frederic
Born in France. Moved to England in the 1890's to work for *The Graphic*. Contributed more than 60 illustrations of the Boer War to that publication. Joined the staff of *The Illustrated London News* in 1910.

Dickinson, F. C.
Known for his black and white illustration done for *The Graphic* and *The Daily Graphic* from 1898 to 1906. More than 50 illustrations of the Boer War done for those two publications. Also known as a watercolorist.

Forestier, Amedee (1854-1930)
Born in Paris, came to London in 1882 to work as staff artist for *The Illustrated London News*. Acted as special artist for the paper until 1899 and covered royal occasions and ceremonies; also "worked up" sketches sent in by other artists. In later life became a noted illustrator of archaeological sites.

Ginko, Adachi
Japanese artist about whose life little is known; his woodblock prints were mainly produced between 1874 and 1900. Especially famous for numerous prints illustrating the Sino-Japan War and the Boxer Rebellion.

Johnson, Herbert (1848-1906)
Lived in London; specialized in illustrations of military subjects and ceremonial occasions. Traveled to India with the Prince of Wales in 1875 to cover the royal visit, and covered military events in Egypt for *The Graphic* in 1882. By 1900 his work most often appeared in *The Daily Graphic*, where he would work from photos and sketches sent from overseas.

Jones, George Kingston (c. 1860-1924 or later)
A London-based illustrator who worked primarily for *The Daily Graphic*. Known for his ability to touch up photographs, and adapt for publication the submission of other artists.

Macpherson, Douglas (1871-1965)
Born in Essex, England, and first trained by his artist father, John Macpherson. Studied at the Westminster School of Art and worked for *The Daily Graphic* and its sister publication, *The Graphic*, from 1890 to 1913, with a number of overseas assignments. In 1913 he joined the staff of *The Sphere* for whom he covered World War I. In 1923 he travelled to Egypt to cover Howard Carter's discovery of Tutankhaman's tomb. Free-lance work during the 1930s and 1940s for various publications.

Matania, Fortunino (1881-1963)

Born in Naples, Italy, where his father was a professor of art. Worked in Milan and Paris before joining the staff of *The Graphic* in 1901. During World War I, served as "Special" correspondent for *The Sphere* and produced hundreds of illustrations of military action.

Nash, Joseph Jr.

Born in London, son of a well-known illustrator with the same name. Started work for *The Graphic* in 1874 and spent his entire working life associated with this publication. Exhibited at the Royal Academy in 1877. Did a number of illustrations of various colonial wars, starting with the Zulu War of 1879.

Radford, Oswald Claude (1850-1924)

Born in England, Radford was a career officer in the British Indian Army who served on the Northwest Frontier of India for 25 years prior to his departure for China in July 1900. His bravery in action in China was recognized in dispatches, and he was named Companion in the Most Eminent Order of the Indian Empire (CIE) in July 1902. He returned to India in 1901 to take part in the Kabul Kheyl Expedition, and retired in 1910.

Soper, George (1870-?)

Born in London, he was known as an etcher, engraver, watercolorist and illustrator. Began to exhibit in London in 1894. Worked for a number of the important magazines and newspapers; was especially well known for his illustrations of the Boer War.

Spence, Percy Frederick Seaton (1868-1933)

Born in Sydney, Australia, and moved to London in 1895 to work as an illustrator for numerous magazines. Began to exhibit at the Royal Academy in 1899. By 1900 was working for *The Graphic*, illustrating the Boer War. From 1905 to 1910 he returned to his native land to work on the publication *Australia*, then returned to London.

Whiting, Fred (or Frederic) (1873-1962)

Born in the London suburb of Hampstead. His education in art included the Royal Academy Art School, St. John's Wood Art School, and the Academie Julian in Paris. While still in training he began to work as an illustrator at *The Graphic* and *The Daily Graphic*. His on-site coverage of the Boxer Rebellion in 1900 and 1901 was so effective that he was sent back to the Far East in February 1904 to cover the Russo-Japan War. He returned to London in 1905 with the Japanese War Medal with Clasp. He became an Associate of the Royal Academy and pursued a serious career in the fine arts. He became a well-known portrait painter and in 1928 joined the staff of the Heatherley School of Art, ultimately becoming Chief Instructor.

Young, P. F.

Known only as a pen and ink illustrator for *The Daily Graphic*.